MEDIEVAL ENGLISH ROMANCE IN CONTEXT

GAIL ASHTON

continuum

Continuum International Publishing Group

The Tower Building 80 Maiden Lane
11 York Road   Suite 704
London SE1 7NX   New York, NY 10038

www.continuumbooks.com

British Library Cataloguing-in-Publication Data
A catalogue record for this book is available from the British Library.

ISBN: 978-1-8470-6249-9 (hardback)
    978-1-8470-6250-5 (paperback)

Library of Congress Cataloging-in-Publication Data
A catalog record for this book is available from the Library of Congress.

Typeset by Newgen Imaging Systems Pvt Ltd, Chennai, India
Printed and bound in Great Britain by CPI Antony Rowe,
Chippenham, Wiltshire

CONTENTS

SERIES EDITORS' PREFACE

Texts and Contexts offers clear and accessible introductions to key literary fields. Each book in the series outlines major historical, social, cultural and literary contexts that impact upon its specified area. It engages contemporary responses to selected texts and authors through a variety of exemplary close readings, by exploring the ideas of seminal theorists and/or a range of critical approaches, as well as examining adaptations and afterlives. Readers are encouraged to make connections and ground further independent study through 'Review, Reading and Research' sections at the end of each chapter which offer selected bibliographies, web resources, open and closed questions, discussion topics and pointers for extended research.

ACKNOWLEDGEMENTS

Heartfelt thanks to Anna Fleming for her belief in this series and continued faith in the face of my prevarications; Fiona McCulloch for her professionalism, easy friendship and sense of humour; Louise Sylvester for her insightful reading, enthusiasm and continued support; and, as ever, to Geoff and Jeanette simply for being there.

INTRODUCTION

What kinds of stories and their authors come to mind when we think of medieval romance? Many of us will have heard of *Sir Gawain and the Green Knight* and the exploits of King Arthur and his Knights of the Round Table. Some may recognize the names of writers like Malory, Marie de France, Chrètien de Troyes, Chaucer, John Gower, Froissart or Machaut perhaps. A few may be aware of romance's intersection with saints' lives, folk and fairy tales, even historiography or chronicles. On the whole, though, a medieval romance tradition consists of a series of largely anonymous works, usually in manuscript form and often held in academic libraries out of the public eye. These texts were gathered into compilations and miscellanies long after they were first written, often for private buyers and collectors and almost all of them with slightly different 'flavours': co-opted for a nationalistic agenda, say, a religious one or simply for ordinary family reading. As such, they all tell us more about the issues and anxieties of a particular time and culture than they do perhaps about their reception when first written. So, too, these manuscripts are subject to the vagaries of time: incomplete, damaged, many of them lost to us altogether.

Yet we know that this was popular fiction with its own cult status just as its afterlives persist today in a variety of forms and media, its motifs, ideas and structures running through a rich and diverse wealth of texts from *Sir Orfeo*, to *Pride and Prejudice* and *Harry Potter*. Romance is a story of origins – not simply a matter of birthright (though we all recognize the archetypal changeling motif) but a consideration of our place in the wider world with its myths, narratives of history, unstable constructions of class, ethnicity and nationhood, and the impulses and effects of colonization. Its focus is on family drama, kinship patterns, the workings out of gender, ideologies of community, leadership, inheritance, on the tension between public and private, time and space. Its worlds are, at once, concrete, ordinary, highly visual and yet strange with parallel dimensions like faery, its slippages of time and space, a crucial element that I call liminal throughout this volume. Here everyday life is distorted and identities are tried on, tested. This is where the real with all its anxieties and social codes is reconfigured, often into a potential utopia, and always through the same motifs: supernatural events or objects; the doubled or shadow self of the monster; significant places and times; bodies of all kinds, including disaggregated ones or those under threat; secrets and outward appearances; stock figures; trajectories of exile and return; love triangles, rivalry and battle or crisis scenes. And at the core of this capacious, long-lived genre is always a potent mix of love, loss and illicit pleasure.

The structure of this book follows the format for the series. Part One attempts to contextualize English romance stories through a brief outline of some of the social, historical and cultural issues of a late medieval world. It examines, too, literary culture and the material production of its manuscripts. Part Two offers a range of critical readings and approaches to several key texts from an English romance tradition: *Sir Gawain and the Green Knight*, *Sir Gowther*, *Lay le Freine*, *Sir Degaré*, *Sir Orfeo*, *Sir Launfal*, *Floris and Blauncheflour*, *Emaré* and the *Man of Law's Tale*, and Malory's *Morte DArthur*.

Part Three begins by discussing some contemporary critical responses to the romance genre, most notably key theorists such as Carolyn Dinshaw, Jeffrey Jerome Cohen, Patricia Clare Ingham and Gilles Deleuze and Félix Guattari. It takes in ideas about gender and queer studies, postcolonialism, concepts of history and the place of theory in medieval studies. Later I examine just a few – *Doctor Who* and its spin-offs, the *Batman* films, Simon Armitage's translation of *Sir Gawain and the Green Knight* – of the many afterlives and adaptations of this compelling genre.

This guide may be used as a dip-in, reference resource (in which case, see the Contents, Index, final resource pages and navigate via the subheadings in each chapter) and/or read in full. It is not a monograph; hence its discussions and interpretations are not comprehensive. There is no singular through-line of argument, though my inclinations and ideas are, I think, clear and cohesive. Lines of inquiry mesh and compete in equal measure; they falter, peter out, circle in, out and around in an attempt to offer starting points, stimulate debate and spark independent research. Similarly, my approach is to track in, out and between extracts and key scenes rather than work a text at a time, in keeping with my focus on the contingent, provisional and profoundly intertextual nature of the romance stories I discuss. Above all, I take a mere handful of the stories of the last 600 or 700 years in an attempt to bear witness to the insistent dialogue between past and present, and to the productive connections between medieval romance and the popular fiction of today.

PART ONE

CONTEXTS

CHAPTER 1

SOCIAL AND CULTURAL CONTEXT

SOCIAL UPHEAVAL

Medieval society is often classified into three estates. After royalty, the most privileged class composed the clergy, nobles and knights. Bottom of the heap was the 'gentils' or the commons – anyone from craftsmen and free landholders (sometimes called the bourgeoisie or the emerging middle class) right down to peasants attached, feudal-style, to aristocratic households. At the same time, as with the rest of Europe, the power of the Catholic Church remained all-pervasive. Ecclesiastical courts were separate from civic ones and dealt with matters large and small, from heresy to proscriptions on birth, marriage and death. Church teachings and writings suffused literary and everyday culture. The medieval year was structured by a liturgical calendar full of saints' days and festivals. Canonical time, with its call to prayer and its bells, measured a medieval 'working' day. The Church was also a feudal overlord, owner of more than a third of all land in England upon which it demanded rent and tithes.

Yet the medieval world was far less static than this commonly accepted overview suggests. Internal power struggles and increased criticism of its practices divided the Church and resulted in the Papal Schism of 1378–1417. Religious reformers like John Wyclif and his 'Lollard' followers campaigned for a devolvement of power from the priest to ordinary people. On the Continent, a raft of similar movements undermined Church authority and would later prompt a crackdown in the form of the Inquisition. Language became a highly charged issue. In spite of its lack of status as a largely oral form, the vernacular was increasingly the language of choice. Wyclif, for example, demanded bibles written in English so that everyone could access Church teachings.

At the same time, Black Death ravaged Europe and led to profound social and economic change. The first wave of this highly virulent pandemic – probably a mix of pneumonic and bubonic plague – hit England in 1348 to kill at least a third of its entire population. The population of London, for instance, halved to around 50,000. Recent research indicates that in specific villages or parts of England up to three-quarters of its people died. Other outbreaks occurred in 1361–62, 1369 and 1375 with sporadic occurrences across Europe for several hundred years after. Though less severe than the first, these later incidences seemed to target children and adolescents in particular. The result was to intensify social upheaval. Labour was scarce. Some noble families were wiped out and/or their line of inheritance (father to son) disrupted. Birth rate fell. Plague hastened the end of England's feudal system and aggravated social changes already under way. The population shifted from rural to urban areas as people sought improved wages and working conditions and manufacturing trades expanded, with especial demand for English textiles. Labour laws of 1349, 1351 and 1361 attempted to freeze wages at pre-plague levels even as a scarcity of labour made it a workers' market. Laws passed in 1349, 1376 and 1388 made letters of permission from feudal lords a requirement for those trying to leave their villages or manors and refused such migrants charitable aid; many of them were fined for vagrancy. In 1381, in protest against this kind of coercion and the exorbitant poll taxes demanded by Richard II to fund his campaigns against the French and the Scots, rebels marched into London in what is known as the Peasants' Revolt. The protest was quickly crushed but 100 years later there were no more serfs left in England.

Perhaps the most dynamic social group in England in the aftermath of the Black Death was the gentils. The 1379 English poll tax sought to define this amorphous group by subdividing it. The highest consisted of esquires and gentlemen in service or chamber knights in royal service; in other words, those with some money and power or loosely aligned with chivalry in the sense of having access to the king. Lesser categories comprised attorneys, aldermen, sergeants, franklins, merchants, pardoners and summoners: essentially those without land or *inherited* money. The gentils were increasingly influential. Its members were often associated with London and, therefore, centralized government, perhaps via economic links with the court or parliament at Westminster, or through ecclesiastical ties (the Archbishop of Canterbury, head of the English Church, resided at Lambeth Palace). However, 'gentils' remains a highly charged term perhaps best defined by its status as respectable rather than feudal. Even so, it redefined aristocratic privilege. Yeomen, for example, achieved particular success as strategic bowmen in the Hundred Years War with France. On their return in the fourteenth and fifteenth centuries, large numbers of them found themselves socially upwardly mobile through their popularity as retainers in noble households. Conversely, many who would previously have been knights in old-style feudal service were now demoted to the lesser ranks of esquire and gentlemen as landowners closed ranks in what was to prove an unsustainable attempt to preserve aristocratic integrity.

Opportunities for social mobility were quickly taken by the gentils who were key players in the transformation of the social face of medieval England. With their increased prosperity, they bought books written in English, and bought or married into land left vacant by failures of dynasty. In this they were aided by a shift in emphasis in canon law, which now preached the importance of individual consent in marriage, proof of sexual consummation and the idea of marriage as a sacrament. Increasingly, the Church ranked these issues alongside older values of kinship and estate, though, in practice, marriage was neither a free choice nor a dynastic, arranged coupling, but somewhere between the two.

NATIONHOOD AND IDENTITIES

Many people forget that medieval England was also a colony under Norman rule since the conquest of 1066 and struggling to define itself both against, and through, its colonized state. London was a melting-pot of French, Norman-French, Flemish, Italian and other European and eastern diplomats, traders and merchants. Internally, 'Britain' continued to be disputed on its Scottish, Welsh and Irish borders. Within England, the dominance of London as the centre of government and commerce meant that 'outside' – the provinces and the north-west especially – was marginalized. This lack of cohesion was exacerbated by the fact that no common language united medieval England. Its official language was French, used alongside Latin for all legal or administrative documents and correspondence. French was spoken in the royal court. In the provinces, Anglo-Norman French still mingled with a non-standard, multiple-dialect English vernacular with no real history – and hence authority – of transcription. Yet as a certain consciousness about 'nation' began to emerge, the vernacular became the language of choice. Its use called up all kinds of vested political, linguistic and cultural agendas; indeed, at times, it might be said to be a dangerous choice.

Both the crusades and the Hundred Years War contributed to social tensions and emerging ideas about nationhood that feed into medieval romance texts. Edward II's claim to the duchy of Aquitaine via his mother's line sparked a war with France that lasted from 1337 to 1453. English successes were numerous to begin with. The French king, Jean II, was captured, for example, and taken to the English court in London where he remained as a 'guest' for a number of years. Yet even as the campaign rapidly turned to deadlock and financially crippled the nation, English kings continued to press for the French crown. Edward II assumed the arms and title of 'King of France' in 1340. Henry VI crowned himself king of France in 1431 and continued with this spurious title even though by 1453 more or less every inch of French ground had been lost. Aquitaine remained a particular bone of contention, not least because the Gascons who inhabited this corner of Brittany considered themselves separate from the French. They had their own language and culture and were initially receptive to English claims until Richard II passed on the dukedom of the region to an unpopular John of Gaunt in 1390. Political manoeuvring of this kind was a feature of a war that ebbed and flowed, ran parallel with campaigns against the Scots who fought for their own independence and also seemed to have little adverse effect on cross-cultural and literary exchanges between France and England.

Though the crusades began as an attempt to expand and unify the Christian world, by the late Middle Ages its mixed fortunes meant that campaigns were losing support. The 2nd Crusade of 1148 had failed miserably with the crucial loss of the Holy Land and all its treasures. Then Acre fell in 1291. Acre and Jerusalem had been part of a handful of Christian colonies backed by the support of the Eastern Orthodox Christian Church in an otherwise largely Islamic east. When crusaders captured and ransacked Constantinople in 1204, its success was tempered by the fact that it hastened the final separation of the Orthodox Church and the Catholic Church in the west (Constantinople had been the headquarters of the Eastern branch of Christianity). The Balkans Crusade of 1395 was disastrous for Christian forces, especially the French Burgundy dukes who had favoured it. Yet in August 1480 the great siege of Rhodes was lifted; around 3500 Turkish soldiers died. In return, in the same month, the Turks captured Otranto, sacking the city, killing or taking as slaves its inhabitants and destroying Christian churches. This constant see-saw of power and the huge expense of operations ensured that when, in 1481, Pope Sixtus IV called on all Europe to avenge Otranto the response was measured. The Church had a vested interest in supporting crusades. The Papal Schism of 1378–1417 meant that the Pope's authority as divinely ordained caretaker of Christianity was insecure. First one then two popes were ordained, whilst the Catholic Church's headquarters moved from Rome to Avignon, France. In this context, the Church's eagerness for crusade was a means of reuniting a fragmented Christendom. The Church sold indulgences to raise revenue for professional crusading soldiers. Many countries raised taxes for crusades, especially after the fourteenth century. Yet many powers were reluctant to commit to future campaigns in this period, increasingly viewed as defensive rather than expanding a Christian empire by recapturing Jerusalem. Accordingly, the Church altered its strategy. It encouraged people to offer prayers or financial assistance to crusade armies by declaring that the spiritual rewards for this matched any gained by actual combat. Similarly, it was acceptable to read about crusades in romances or travel writings, for instance.

EAST AND WEST

On the one hand, then, the crusades were part of a drive to expand and secure the Christian world. Yet they point up, too, an increasing late medieval awareness of emerging national, rather than supranational, identities. The English kings Richard II, Henry VI, Edward IV and Henry II all assumed the title 'Most Christian King', even as some of them made parallel claims to French soil. 'Nationhood' revolves around matters of difference to mark off religious, racial or ethnic, linguistic, class and geographical borders, none of which is ever secure. The crusades attempted to assert an east–west division in medieval culture that was in fact far more diffuse. As early as the twelfth century, for instance, Almeria in Spain was a locus for east–west commercial transaction. Reputed for its silks and at the heart of a medieval slave trade, it straddled 'Muslim' Iberia, Syria and Egypt and 'Latin, Christian' Andalucia and Europe. Similarly, famous pilgrimage routes like the Santiago trail tracked through Europe and on into the east to bring together traders and pilgrims from all around the world. Treasures from the east were brought to England by returning crusaders, including translations of texts by Arab scholars. Even the so-called patron saint of England, Saint George, was actually a Turkish knight, part of a festive eastern drama. Eastern cultures share in shaping Europe's history and overspill its borders.

Medieval world maps exemplify some of the problematics of 'east' and what this might mean for a medieval 'west' in general and concepts of nation in particular. Medieval cartographers depicted the world as simultaneously whole and divided. Genealogical connections made through descent from the biblical sons of Noah – Shem, Ham and Japheth – seemed to offer unity. Sometimes their names appear in place of the names of continents: Asia as Shem, Africa as Ham and Europe or the west as Japheth. So, too, the peoples of the world shared a spiritual affinity according to medieval thought, whereby Christ will redeem everyone. The head, hands and feet of Jesus were, thus, often painted on the edges of the known world. Yet the three separate continents or spheres also proposed partition as did the fact that the world was quartered: in four cardinal directions, with four winds and four angels in each of the four corners of the earth, in line with the teachings of Revelations 7:1. Similarly, *mappaemundi* might split the globe into *Oriens* – the top of the map associated with heat, black skin, the sun rising – and the cold, paler-skinned north or *Occidens* where the sun sets. Even these ostensible ethnic or racial characteristics resist stereotype, however, when we see that the maps are actually oriented towards the east and not the west. East takes central position since it has Jerusalem, the goal of those early crusades, at its heart. Thus any equation of an inferior east full of dark-complexioned Arabian or African Muslims or non-Christian infidels is far more ambivalent than first appears; 'East' or the 'Orient' has no fixed correlation. Similarly, romance's frequent deployment of the term 'Saracen' – defined by the Oxford English Dictionary as groups of Arab nomads – interchanges with 'Muslim' or 'infidel' and refers less to a distinct ethnic or religious entity than to a construct, which is but one example of an ongoing narrative about nations and identities.

Medieval attitudes towards Jews further complicate medieval culture. In the eleventh century, crusaders massacred Jews en route to the Holy Land on the grounds of their non-Christianity, including them in the category of 'infidel' in a manner often repeated in literature. Persecution of Jews was a feature of medieval England and Europe for reasons often obscure. Jews were blamed for spreading Black Death, especially as many were itinerant traders and merchants. Other cultural and religious misunderstandings of Jewish faith and culture accreted to give rise to accusations of well poisoning, ritual murder, desecrating the communion wafer in the Christian sacrament of the Eucharist and even cannibalism. These ideas combined with a raft of social upheavals seemingly to justify acts of violence against individual Jews and their communities. A new sense 'Englishness', for instance, saw lands and goods owned by Jews seized and claimed as English by right. English nobles and civic councils tried to interfere with Jewish custom and laws to effect an internal colonization, culminating in the expulsion of all Jews from England in 1290.

The inclusion of Jews in the category of 'east' shifts common perceptions of how medievals viewed their world. At the same time, concerns about Englishness or how to construct nationhood feed into the anxious histories and cultural formations on which such simplistic and unstable binaries turn and find their way into late medieval romance fiction. Where and how might England define its borders given its ambivalent relation to Scotland, Ireland and Wales, let alone to its Norman conquerors, to France, and to the rest of Europe? How do kinship and matters of nation intersect the notion of a unified Christian empire? If 'western' Europe defines itself against an occidental 'East' then where does an insular England fit? If 'east' is culturally, ethnically, economically, even religiously cross-cut by 'west', how does Europe constitute itself?

CONQUEST AND HISTORY

Chivalric romances' peculiar courtly world plays out and disputes an array of social matters pertinent to medieval society. Romance is a genre about nation and nation building. To subdivide it into 'matters of England' or 'matters of nation' imposes a coherent unity that the many historical and political disjunctures of late medieval England deny. Concepts of nation are founded on both external *and* internal threat, as many romance tales testify. The English War of the Roses (1455–87) was a civil war centred on the dynastic claims of two competing aristocratic households, the houses of York and Lancaster. It began in 1399 when Richard II was deposed by Henry Bolingbroke, Duke of Lancaster and, later, Henry IV. From then on, the crown was disputed through the subsequent reigns of Henry V and the infant son who succeeded him in 1432, Henry VI. All-out civil war was still in progress when Malory wrote the *Morte Darthur* from his prison cell (1469–70).

More generally, conquest invariably brings in its wake a crisis of historical continuity centred on narratives about those histories – often represented in a distant past – and also upon language. The Arthurian cycles, in particular, instance this. In 1190, a corpse was exhumed and identified as the legendary Arthur's. These bones were translated to Glastonbury Abbey to become an iconic resting place for Arthur and his Round Table. The event was highly regarded by Henry II who manipulated it to diminish a Welsh claim upon Arthur as the resurrected king who would lead them to independence. Instead, the English seized upon Arthur to create a mythological-historical British Celtic past, even as Wales, Scotland and Ireland claimed him as their own. Increasingly, Arthurian stories settle as part of an English national heritage with the Gawain-tales and other late fourteenth century texts focused on an idyllic Arthurian golden age separate from earlier Saxon invasions and Anglo-Norman rule. Most were composed in the vernacular, a choice that further embeds nationalistic tendencies, and circulated separate from, but parallel to, Arthurian cycles in French, which were more concerned with Lancelot and the search for the Holy Grail as symbols of the highest personal, social and spiritual worth.

At the same time, anti-French hostility induced by the Hundred Years War was countered by a rise in romances written and copied in England about French heroes and their martial success. Yet these so-called Charlemagne romances, despite their title, centre on heroes who are Christian first and French only incidentally. They offer models of Christian unity and military prowess to suggest that romance combines ideas about Englishness, a Christian super-state *and* social or family matters as part of a larger debate about nationhood. Stories about knights, idealized chivalric communities and courtly love scenarios are the stuff of popular romance despite their increasing distance from late medieval world-views. These set-pieces and motifs probably offered a safe space in which to play out contemporaneous issues such as dynastic inheritance and marriage, social ties and identities, and noble birth versus personal merit. Many romances turn upon clashes of consent and desire, on questions of succession, *gentillesse* or kinship, on incest or rape averted and failures of dynasty like adulterous or childless marriages. So, the Arthur-Guinevere-Lancleot triangle brings down the Round Table fellowship; Chaucer's 'Wife of Bath's Tale' in *The Canterbury Tales* reworks a 'Lothly-lady' folk motif as an argument about *gentillesse*; a Saracen king abducts the wife of *Sir Isumbras*; *Floris and Blauncheflour* asserts mutual love and consent over force and matters of birthright. *Sir Degrevant*, too, exemplifies this 'new' social world in which the prosperous protagonist, and careful guardian of his own and his tenants' welfare, tries to marry up and out of his class. The tale's careful detailing of property and its rights and restorations – fences, hunting permits, a deer park, rivers, farms, wagons, horses, seed – crystallize Degravant's worth in contrasts to the Earl's birth and flagrant lack of social responsibility.

CHAPTER 2

LITERARY CONTEXT AND MATERIAL CULTURE

LANGUAGE

Though medieval romances were popular in Anglo-Norman and in French, English romance text production – including an outpouring of London-based miscellanies – exploded in the years between 1390 and 1410. Clearly something crucial was at stake in the language chosen for these fictions. In order to grasp the full implications of what was increasingly an issue for all medieval writing, we need to step back and reconsider the circulation of languages at this time. Three languages were in use in the medieval period. Latin, the most prestigious tongue, was used for all ecclesiastical and scholarly matters. Its choice aligns with the Church, with power and ancient 'histories'. At the same time, French was the official language of England. Two forms were employed concurrently. Courtly, aristo-cratic French was the language of law, government, diplomacy and an élite ruling class. It was invested, too, with the power of the colo-nizer in the later years of French rule over England. The second form was Anglo-Norman, the mother tongue of the 1066 conquerors, which, though inferior in status to the French spoken in royal circles, was used far more readily, especially in the provinces. There it co-mingled with England's third and least regarded language, English.

The English vernacular was the language of the English people, though to use the singular to describe what was, in fact, a disparate array of groups and regions, each with its own dialect or mode of English, is somewhat misleading. Unlike French and Latin – but more like Anglo-Norman – English was a spoken language. As such, it lacked both the stability and status of written languages. Instead, it was a language subject to, and indicative of, change. This was because medieval English was fluid and non-standard in form, incorporating shifts in dialect and a host of words from other languages, such as French. It was, too, the tongue of the 'commons' or 'gentils'. This means that it was not only widely spoken, but part of the shifting status of that social group brought about by the impact of Black Death, as well as the material fact of the invention of the printing press, for example, which led to increased literacy. Above all, English was a pre-conquest language, in part a rejection of French, Anglo-Norman colonial power and so potentially, at least, a language of dissent and transformation.

In the late Middle Ages, English authors like Geoffrey Chaucer and John Gower, plus a host of often anonymous romance writers, chose it for their published works. The 1362 parliament confessed that its proceedings were increasingly conducted in English rather than French, as was traditional. Accordingly, it passed a statute permitting the conduct of all court matters in English since, it added, no one understood French. The parliaments of 1363, 1364 and 1381 all opened in English. Henry III was confirmed in English as well as French, while, from 1417 until his death, Henry V used the vernacular in almost all of his correspondence with government and cities outside London. The issue of language is, then, central to the circulation and meaning of medieval texts, especially romances.

The word 'romance' is derived from Old French '_mettre en romanz_', meaning to translate into the vernacular (in this case into French). Early romances translated Latin epics and chronicles into French, or, to be more precise, into Anglo-Norman. But the process of translation in medieval culture is a complex one, not least because the Middle English meaning of 'to translate' is 'translate or _transform_.' Many of these early Anglo-Norman romances circulated in England in the twelfth-century court of Henry II and Eleanor of Aquitaine. Different manuscript versions of the same tale reveal how varying accounts move across and between different audiences, cultures and languages or dialects. What might have been a straightforward translation into Anglo-Norman may well become an entirely different story once it is copied and circulated in English, say, or Spanish or Italian. Equally, the non-standard nature of a vernacular like English compounds the process of transmission in its own time _and_ adds to contemporary difficulties in approaching extant medieval romances; unlike Chaucer's 'English' which was centred on London and the south-east and became the English of today, romances were written in all dialects, including less prestigious ones such as northern or the north-west midlands/Cheshire tongue of the anonymous Gawain poet. Language or dialect, genre and content are all seemingly on the move in medieval romance works, a fluidity reflected too in the unique shape of its stories and its shape-shifting motifs, disguises, doublings, reversals and journeys. Thus to translate is a process that transforms, energizes rather than spoils an 'original' that given the nature of medieval manuscript culture never really exists in the first place.

MEDIEVAL MANUSCRIPTS

Language is not the only issue at stake in medieval literary texts. Writing and translating, copying, compiling and circulating texts occur in a number of different contexts: social, literary, cultural, political, aesthetic or intellectual. Each of the processes just mentioned is affected too by the material means of its (textual) production. Medieval manuscripts (where most medieval romances are found) are physically different from modern books and print. Written in unfamiliar English (or Old French, Anglo-Norman and so on), they are also non-standard with no common orthography, spelling or punctuation. Lines and pages are rarely numbered. They have no recognizable critical or academic framework in the sense of footnotes or endnotes, an index, bibliography, glossary, introduction or explanatory notes. Many scripts lack a title page or even, in some instances, a title. Most probably the work(s) will be unsigned with few clues about its author or authors. The style and content of the same story will vary from version to version. Thus our own contemporary reading maps will be of only limited use in helping us to read.

Age and preservation of a manuscript may further exacerbate these difficulties. Pieces may be missing, altered and/or annotated and its copy illegible in places. All manuscripts were written out by hand by a scribe or scribes working on vellum and to order, from the author's exemplar script. Scribes actively altered texts as they copied them, often contributing to the eventual destruction of their fragile working materials. Sometimes this was through error or misreading. At others, it was deliberate: to censor certain passages or ideas or to call attention to them, often as a response to the scribe's own literary or philosophical leanings; as a means of pleasing or avoiding offence to a patron commissioning the copy; or, particularly later on with the advent of more professional copying services, perhaps because of the need to edit these bespoke, expensive manuscripts to a certain size or shape (most were 24 pages or so). As manuscripts circulated, so, too, other readers might annotate the text. Medieval readers navigated texts in ways entirely different from our own. Most manuscripts are illustrated. They contain markers and codices like pointing fingers or fabulous beasts, or have other *marginalia*, including additions and embellishments. All of these call attention to aspects of the story or to contentious or key ideas and sequences. These are visual clues on how to read, including literally in the sense of which comes first, which next (not necessarily linear). Above all, these cue a certain kind of reading that privileges parts of a text and, thus, points to particular interpretations. In other words, illuminations, comments and *marginalia* provide both literal and critical maps for reading. Clearly, then, medieval writing was a collaborative process with input from a variety of audiences and plenty of opportunity for change and corruption of manuscripts. Without a static text, and in an age that prized scholarship over originality – hence the numerous references in medieval works to source material and other authors – modern notions of copyright and authorial authority disappear.

Other differences between contemporary and medieval text production impact on our reading. Print-based texts tend to lose impact through repetition. In contrast, oral cultures accrue formulaic structures and cues; these aid memory, add appeal by keeping listeners attentive and signal switches of scene or tone. Minstrels may have performed and improvised early romances; certainly the French *chansons de gestes* form has some overlap with romance. Yet there is no simple or linear transition from oral to print culture. Rather, the two were concurrent. Medieval written texts of all kinds were *transitional* texts and thus bear the traces of oral performance: reference to a narrator, perhaps, who may or may not describe himself as the author, to named patrons or to a listening audience, with terms such as 'Herkneth', and written in verse to aid recall.

By the end of the fourteenth century, romance stories were increasingly in prose, indicating a move towards more stable, less fluid 'print' texts. At the same time, prose romances began to develop the interlaced structures we so often associate with the genre today and easily recognized in Victorian serialized novels and film or TV dramas, especially soap operas. Interlacing involves scene-switching, multiple plot lines or deferred endings, which are all the hallmarks of more complex print forms. It also allows for the contraction or expansion of scenes during a performance in response to audience demands, or else for the privileging of certain figures or elements of the story. Such features are equally the hallmarks of more performative or 'oral' cues. Thus the transition from oral storytelling to print was probably far less linear or simple than some scholars suggest.

The particular manuscript history of romance suggests that its transmission was also far more complex than other medieval forms. Even these first prose romances were often still heavily decorated. In part, this may simply reiterate that medieval culture remained a memorial culture. *Memoria* is not simply about memory – though the ability to recite by heart was considered a sign of genius and moral worth. Rather, *memoria* is the term given to the technology of remembering. Just as repetition is one means of enabling the process of recall, so, too, is illustration and decoration of manuscripts. Yet there are more visual cues in Middle English romances overall than in any other genre. The fact of these extra navigational aids tends to support the view of some scholars that romance remains especially resistant to the shaping and defining effect that print has on most other genres. Instead, the loose and hybrid form of romance keeps it transformative and transitional, qualities that, in part, account too for its vigorous afterlife in modern culture. Romance manuscripts are also especially marked by oral performance. In addition to the usual invocations and addresses to its audiences, romance stories often have artificial start and end points in the form of prologues or *incipits*, epilogues and *explicits*, prayers and titles. Other performative footholds common to all stories retold from memory are particularly numerous in romance. Indeed, they seem to define the genre: formulaic structures, cipher-characters, repetitions, set-piece scenes, recurring motifs and spectacular moments or details. Equally, the borrowing from other stories and other texts, even those in different vernaculars – again, usual in all medieval works – is especially strong in romance where it seems to have two functions: to work as mnemonic aid *and* to flag an increasingly self-reflexive intertextuality (whereby stories call attention to the ways in which they repeat and connect) that holds true even today.

ATTRIBUTION AND AUDIENCES

The complex context of medieval manuscript production ensured that writers, readers, editors and compilers, copy-scribes and commissioning patrons all played a part in its material culture. Accordingly, it is rare to find an author's name on any medieval manuscript, but, once again, romances seem especially susceptible to this lack of attribution. Instead, we are far more likely to be able to identify place of origin (often via its dialect) and, sometimes, a connection with other manuscript compilations. Even where a name is recorded, the unique nature of medieval manuscript culture means that it could belong to a compiler, an editor or a scribe as much as to the writer of a particular text. A name on a script may also be that of its dedicatee.

Attribution of medieval romances is, thus, either multi-layered or impossible. Even the signing of an author's name may be fraught with difficulties. To name may be less an accurate attribution than a construct that tells us something of the tensions within the literary circles and courtly culture to which it corresponds. Other material facts influence both the production and reception of medieval romance. Though many of it stories centre on aristocratic or chivalric life, this was popular fiction, then as well as now. We still have copies of over 100 romances written in English, testimony to its status as possibly the most widely read genre in medieval culture. French and English verse romances were re-worked into prose across the fifteenth century. Some of those same stories find their way into plays and popular ballads. Certainly they circulated throughout medieval England, France, Germany, Italy, Spain, Greece, Portugal and the Netherlands. The newly literate, socially mobile bourgeoisie enjoyed these stories as much as anyone but the lucrative market they provided for these vernacular texts was also a consciously political manoeuvre. In addition, provincial readers and listeners – the rural gentry of fourteenth century England, for example, as well as burgesses, merchants and craftsmen – gained access to these works thanks to a more commercial printing enterprise. Evidence within romance manuscripts themselves verifies that women were an important and growing influence on romance consumption. Notable collectors include the aforementioned Marie de Champaigne and her mother Eleanor of Aquitaine. Both noble and bourgeois library collections show women reading and patronizing romance. Scholars generally agree that romance makes up the second largest genre of literature owned or circulated specifically by women, a state that continues long after many of these texts were initially compiled.

The popularity of romance is perhaps best accounted for as what Nicola McDonald aptly terms "collective fiction". This assumes a community of listeners/readers who enter into it via their shared knowledge of its codes – its repetitions, its borrowings and structures, all of which contribute to its pleasure (McDonald, 2000: 14). With romance, as with popular forms like detective or other genre fiction, an audience knows what to expect. Enjoyment stems in part from adherence to these codes and/or their manipulation, hence its self-reflexive in-jokes. The question of romance's particular appeal to women – including to writers like Marie de France and a host of modern female authors – is more difficult to gauge. Did they allow women access to a literary culture they were formerly denied? These are stories told in the mother tongue or vernacular. They focus on family, kinship, marriage, lineage and property, all social and political structures in which the stakes for women have traditionally been high and to which women are paradoxically both central *and* marginal. This double-bind is perpetuated in later academic denigration of romance as 'women's fiction', an issue to which I return in Part Three.

PROVENANCE: ORIGINALITY AND COMPILATION

As I have already indicated, the notion of an authentic or original text mass-produced in book form and complete with authorial copyright and attribution was anathema to medieval culture. As well as overcoming this cultural hurdle to negotiate the complex maze of medieval textual production, modern readers face an additional dilemma when confronted with romance manuscripts. Single copies are relatively rare; like other medieval writings, most were compiled into loosely organized folio-style miscellanies. So romance 'collections' comprise epic, didactic, chronicle, travel writings, historiography and romance texts all in one. What adds to the problem for contemporary audiences is the lack of recognizable authors – and hence an emerging canon of works – and the gap between the so-called romance originals (especially difficult to identify for all the reasons outlined earlier) and the text that is now in a compilation or miscellany.

Most romances survive in compilations that gather them up anything up to 200 years after the estimated date of their composition. In part, this large gap can be attributed to the advent of new print technologies, which prompted an explosion of copying of all kinds of texts, especially in the fifteenth century. We can certainly identify and date some individual vernacular romances. Equally we have access to a number of extant manuscript compilations. We know, for instance, of around fifty chivalric metrical (verse) romances written in English. In the main, these were taken from French sources and composed between 1250 or so and the early 1500s. They exist in various versions across ninety late medieval manuscripts and in a few printed fragments up into the sixteenth century. Other works include three manuscripts of *King Horn* (one in Anglo-Norman), which is believed to be the earliest English romance in existence. We generally date *Havelok* to the end of the thirteenth century and think it is from Lincolnshire. A full version of *Richard Coeur de Lion* was composed in English in the south midlands around 1300. *Sir Gawain and the Green Knight* was written in the late fourteenth century in the northwest midlands (Cheshire). *Sir Launfal* is extant in a single manuscript dating from the early fourteenth century and, for once, we know its author: Thomas le Chestre. The version appears in the fifteenth century Cotton Caligula Aii compilation currently held in the British Museum, London; as such, it offers compelling evidence of the textual gap that occurs in many romances still available to us. Similarly, three versions of *Sir Orfeo* survive, in different compilations from different times: in Harley 3810 and Ashmole 61 – both fifteenth century – and in the fourteenth century Auchlineck collection.

There are many other examples. *Sir Isumbras*, probably written in the 1330s, has less of a time lag with appearances in collections in 1350 and in others well into the 1400s. Two versions of *Sir Gawain and the Carl of Carlisle* seem to have circulated according to scholarly investigation but only one late medieval copy remains in MS Parkington 10. In contrast, four manuscripts of *Floris and Blauncheflour* survive, most incomplete; the fullest versions are in MS Egerton and the Auchlineck collections. Similarly, there are four extant copies of *Sir Eglamour*, one in the famous Thornton compilation and then with new copies produced right up until the 1570s. Like *Sir Launfal*, the Middle English version of *Lay le Freine* seems to be based on Marie de France's twelfth century 'original'. Again, the manuscript is incomplete and so dating it is problematic: many academics suggest 1330. Scholars also believe that it was written by the same poet who composed *Sir Orfeo* in English. Each shares the same prologue, though this may simply mean that the same scribe copied out both stories.

Information of this kind recurs in many academic essays and modern anthologies. On its own, it is at best superfluous and at worse misleading. What the above list demonstrates is actually how little we know about the provenance of most medieval romances. What it *does* reveal, though, is something far more crucial, namely the unique context of their material production, without which any attempt to read or historicize an individual romance may well narrow perspective, in my view.

COMPILATION AND MANUSCRIPT

It is highly unlikely that modern scholarship will uncover the original source of a particular romance. Rather, we perhaps need to focus less on patchy attempts at attribution and far more on competing versions of the same story that circulates *variously*: abridged, amplified, with sections interchanged or repeated, with or without deliberate or otherwise scribal workings and *marginalia*. Above all, we would do well to recall that medieval texts are collaborative enterprises whereby contexts shift and the players in each – audience, writer, compiler, scribe, patron – all contribute to the making of meaning. Contemporary reception of these works also replicates this process to some extent. That is because medieval romances often construct what we *think* is an authentic Middle English version suitable for publication in the twenty-first century. Who decides this and how are modern editions compiled?

Academic scholarship has a vested interest in preserving such texts in a particular form, usually one suitable for study and often in an 'original' language that limits their circulation. It will choose one or more manuscripts as a base text, judged, rightly or wrongly, to be authentic archive material close to an impossible original. Yet a manuscript's survival does not tell the whole story about its impact in medieval culture. The number of extant manuscripts, for example, is not such an obvious clue about a story's popularity as might appear. Nor does it offer any real indication about its network of affiliation to other romances. We know, for instance, that the tale of *Emaré* belongs to a type of oft-repeated (therefore presumably popular) story known as the Accursed or Exiled Queens Saga, and that it has many analogues. *Emaré* survives, though, in a single compilation, the Cotton Caligula Aii. With it is a typical miscellany of other poems of all kinds which give us no real flavour or clue about its clearly complex intersection with other texts. The anonymous verse romance the *Tale of Gamelyn*, however, lives on in some twenty-five manuscripts. At first sight, this would signal a huge appeal. Yet *Gamelyn* is part of Chaucer's *The Canterbury Tales* apocryphal canon (those stories said to be by Chaucer but not) and so hangs on to the coattails of one of the few 'named' medieval authors thus skewing its popular appeal. Just to compound the issue, though, its analogues frequently appear in medieval and early modern *Robin Hood* cycles.

Modern-day editorial choices inevitably involve, too, questions of literary taste or aesthetic judgement, as well as a host of other issues. Do we simply transcribe a document or perform our own modern-day scribal transaction on it by cleaning it up, modernizing its spelling or orthography, working through a selection of different manuscripts and taking pieces from each, perhaps? Should editors work alone or in collaboration? What happens when we impose contemporary print practices and technologies – including web-based or digital media – upon medieval texts? Do we enhance, alter or detract from meaning? Do we widen or restrict any (original) popular appeal? Modern readings are always retrospective with most romances extant from their date of *compilation* rather than composition. Ought we then to recreate a context for each romance by examining as many versions and hypothetical readings as possible?

Around three-fifths of all extant romances of the thirteenth and fourteenth centuries appear in just four miscellanies. Auchinleck, Advocates 19.3.1 was copied in the second half of the 1300s and is currently held in the National Library of Scotland. The others were all collated in the 1400s: Cotton Caligula Aii held in the British Library, London, the CUL Ff.2.38 in Cambridge University Library and the Lincoln Cathedral Library MS91, more commonly known as the Thornton MS after the Yorkshire gentleman who commissioned it somewhere between 1430 and 1440. As with all miscellanies, romances sit alongside religious and secular tales, chronicles, saints' lives and travel writings but each has its own distinctive flavour. The London-based Auchinleck has *Bevis of Hampton, Kyng Alisaunder, Floris and Blauncheflour*, *King Richard* and *the King of Tars* alongside stories of 'eastern' saints like Catherine of Alexandria and Margaret of Antioch; a cursory glance at this list might encourage a reading based on east/west divisions and a concern about nationhood. CUL Ff 2.38 is more provincial in tone. Collated in Leicestershire in the 1480s, its narrative range is wide with *Sir Degaré, Bevis of Hampton*,

Guy of Warwick, Le Bone Florence of Rome and others. These tales too are mostly in simple tail-rhyme or four-stress couplets rather than the more sophisticated five-stress line used by Chaucer. One inference, then, is that this collection, with its emphasis on kinship and lineage, was compiled for a bourgeois audience.

Clearly the business of compilation demanded a series of aesthetic, professional and critical judgements. The fact that it is rare to find a compilation of a single author, even where the work is signed, as with Chaucer or Chrétien de Troyes, indicates that these miscellanies were commissioned by families and households for their devotion and amusement. At the same time, modern criticism of romance's formulaic structures is partly accounted for by the professionalization of scribal and editing services that accompanies the advent of the printing press. Copying on demand, and often having to cut time and costs, means that borrowing and replication of material increases. That so many romances share similarities points, too, to a standard or bestselling list of stories.

Equally, the quality of each compilation reveals something of its readership. The Auchinleck, Cotton Caligula Aii and the CUL Ff 2.38 are all professional collaborations between scribes, London printers and booksellers (the abbreviations of the titles usually refer to where the manuscript was either found or is now held, and the numbers to the various processes of editing it for modern consumption). Auchinleck has a series of miniature illustrations, indicating that this was an expensive bespoke design for a private patron. In contrast, the Thornton MS collates material from a variety of sources over a length of time, presumably as it becomes available. This is typical of manuscripts copied by and between families and friends. As publishing became more professional, it became increasingly difficult to ascertain exactly who had input into a manuscript. Some say that scribes continued to copy and compile. Others suggest that editors and compilers were more likely to have been educated men such as clerics (Putter, 2000: 4–7).

More and more, then, medieval texts were customized to the individual tastes of those commissioning them. The effect that this had upon the organization and content of miscellanies also offers clues about their reading and early critical reception. Some compilations are, as I have indicated, more mixed than others, but each has a distinctive flavour through which we might guess something of the ways in which medieval readers make meaning of them. For instance, many French manuscripts begin with stories of Troy and classical Greece and move on to Arthurian cycles. Yet the inclusion of such tales in these miscellanies suggests more about an emerging, late medieval sense of nationhood – authenticated by defining a vernacular history through a lost Arthurian idyll – than anything of literary history or development.

INTERTEXTUALITY

The profoundly intertextual nature of medieval romance is another issue modern readers need to bear in mind. The recurrence of certain stories, figures, motifs and other elements is, as we have already seen, both a result of medieval material culture *and* of romance's formulaic structures – themselves a hangover from oral performance and part of a shift into print. Such repetition also occurs in contemporary cult romances like *Star Trek, Dr Who* and *Lord of the Rings*. As such, it highlights, too, the ways in which intertextuality contributes towards ensuring popular status.

Perhaps the best example of this is the special place that Arthurian legends seem to hold in romance. Geoffrey of Monmouth's *History of the Kings of Britain* was widely copied across England and the Continent to become a seminal text; 220 copies of it remain today. Its derivatives include Wace's highly popular *Roman du Brut* (1150) in which Arthur's Round Table appears for the first time, and Laȝamon's *Brut*, an early thirteenth century poem (and the second longest verse in the entire English canon at over 16,000 lines). Unlike the more spiritually inspired Arthurian cycles in French, Monmouth's *History* and its followers simultaneously offered a wish-fulfilment fantasy of national 'British' unity yet seemed to resonate with disparate groups within that concept. Monmouth's history is a construction that incorporates a folk memory still alive for native Celts of the time. He recalls Merlin's prophecy that a direct descendant of Britain's mythical founding-father, Brutus (a Trojan exile), will one day return to rule. This mythology denies the fact of the Saxon conquest of England and bypasses, too, a Norman conquest of 1066 that still held in medieval England. Paradoxically, it also justifies that conquest; there William saves the nation from the Saxons who are deemed unfit to rule. In this way, the same story might also provide a foundation narrative for Anglo-Normans. Thus Arthur becomes an icon for Englishness and emerging concepts of nationhood, something to which both the *Alliterative* and *Stanzaic* 'Arthurs' (c.1400 and c.1350s, respectively) and Malory's *Morte Darthur* return (1469–70, printed by Caxton in 1485).

Caxton's 1485 edition of Malory's prose romance pitches Arthur as a real historical figure, something, he says, that Welsh and French versions recognized long before this incursion of the legend into English for the first time. In addition, the context of the work, which was written during England's civil War of the Roses, attempts to place it as an exemplary model of leadership and national stability (stability is one of Malory's key words, especially in the closing books), despite the impact of social change on a nobility that was no longer 'pure' and guaranteed by lineage. Rather, this class was composed of nobles, gentils, esquires, knights, many of whom were no longer fighting men but administrators who probably bought, rather than inherited, their land, titles or coats of arms. In one sense, then, Malory's Arthurian ideal is an outdated, nostalgic retrospective for an England without a proper birth story.

The first complete Arthurian story is probably Chrétien de Troyes' *Erec et Enide* (c.1160). This was followed by an outpouring of Arthurian stories in many different styles and settings, especially in the thirteenth century. In the *Conte du Graal*, for instance, de Troyes recounts what appears to have been the inspirational story of the interweaving quests of Perceval and Gawain across some 9,000 verses before ending in mid-sentence. Numerous re-workings follow this account, including four actual continuations. Arthurian stories form a particular subset of medieval romance with many features in common: familiar motifs like Excalibur, recurrent figures from Merlin to Morgan le Fay, Lancelot to Guinevere, and certain settings such as Carlisle or Carleon in Wales. Stories about Gawain were especially popular in England. These seem to begin with *Sir Gawain and the Green Knight* in around 1380 and include a host of analogues and other versions like *The Wedding of Sir Gawain and Dame Ragnell*, *The Turk and Gawain* and *The Carl of Carlisle*. The Gawain cycle shares a number of structures. Arthur's often youthful court is challenged in the midst of a festival or an occasion like a royal hunt. The interloper is a familiar medieval 'other': a giant and/or a green man, a freakish woman or hag, a Turk. This outsider often turns out to be related to Arthur or his court and so is a doubled figure. Further, the Gawain stories in particular are often northern in flavour or setting. *Sir Gawain and the Green Knight* is set on the borders of Lancashire,

Cheshire, and Derbyshire whilst others are set in Carlisle, Cumbria or the Scottish borders, perhaps to foreground their capacity for disruption. What is particularly significant is the way in which all the tales interconnect. The challenger of *The Turk and Gawain* is Sir Gromer, brother of Dame Ragnell who is the bride in *The Wedding of Sir Gawain and Dame Ragnell*. He is also the same Sir Gromer who sets a trap for Gawain in *The Wedding* story and who, in some Arthurian analogues, allies with Mordred to bring down Arthur and his Round Table.

How important is this intertextuality for present-day readings? In the Arthurian and Gawain cycles, the same systems are under scrutiny with similar pleasures and anxieties about food, chivalry, gender and kinship. Yet popular figures recur differently in these analogues and retellings. Gawain, for instance, has a unique fictional history that tracks through vernacular romances. He appears in the *Stanzaic Morte Arthur*, the *Alliterative Morte Arthure* and Malory's later prose *Morte Darthur*, as well as the Welsh *Mabinogion* and other Celtic texts. In addition, he plays a part in a host of European cycles, especially twelfth- and thirteenth-century French and Anglo-Norman ones like *Lancelot* or *Perceval*. Gawain also plays a central role in Geoffrey of Monmouth's *History of the Kings of Britain*. There he is a warrior and defender of Arthur, his uncle and liege lord of his fellow Round Table knights. Mostly, though not exclusively, Gawain is depicted as an ideal of perfect courtesy that appeals to both men and women. In some tales he even has superhuman strength that waxes and wanes with the sun. Yet other romances play on these emblematic qualities. In *Sir Gawain and the Green Knight*, for instance, the Lady demands Gawain's name and teases him, and his medieval audience, with prior knowledge of his repute as a lady's man that the young and rather naïve Gawain of the poem has yet to achieve. All too often, though, contemporary audiences read *Sir Gawain and the Green Knight* as a stand-alone text divorced from its rich inter-textual context, and so may miss undercurrents and generic subtleties appreciated by contemporaneous readers and listeners.

HYBRIDITY

Earlier, I described how the extraordinarily capacious nature of romance is yet another factor in its reading. Twelfth-century chronicle writers like Geoffrey of Monmouth introduced stories about

England's alleged island past which often centred on King Arthur to give us a mythical history frequently taken up by writers of romance. In turn, figures from these early romance stories – often called 'insular romances' – crossed over into chronicles where they were invested as 'fact'. Both chroniclers and romance authors shared stories, intermingled styles and between them constructed a history of England. Equally, they validated their work in similar ways, often sharing patrons, using epilogues and prologues and 'knowledge' of the past as a value-laden idyll with lessons for present. Other texts such as the *Sege of Melayne* or the *Emaré* analogues are hybrids of romance and hagiography, sometimes with a dash of chronicle 'history' too. They remain secular stories but frequently contain a moral message. Some fall into the category of penitential romance, according to some academics, on account of their motifs of divine or miraculous intervention and a central protagonist's penance for his or her failures. Alternatively they may be more obviously devotional, chivalric stories such as those in the Arthurian cycles that focus on the search for the Holy Grail. More importantly, most stories recur in different forms and versions to mingle all kinds of possibilities and defy classification altogether.

Individual romances are, then, frequently generically unstable, something compounded by the miscellaneous nature of most of the compilations in which they appear. The unique flavour of each medieval miscellany points up entirely different ways of reading the same text. This mixing of forms indicates that medieval editing and publication processes were entirely different from our own and, even, that medieval audiences may not have 'read' romances as romance at all. Romance's resistance to classification is paradoxically what keeps it alive, even as it obscures its provenance. Modern editions often compile romances on the basis of so-called manuscript evidence to give us a series of best-fit stories. Additionally, many then subdivide them into categories for ease of reference. In so doing, the tales become fixed in ways that may run counter both to their medieval contexts and to the nature of romance altogether. So, when a scholar like Donald Sands (1986) identifies a group as 'Matter of England', he gathers up a loosely connected set of stories that have no central figure or family network of affiliation – as in Arthurian cycles – *and* contentiously implies a distinct point of stability for medieval 'England'.

Each compilation, medieval or contemporary, is, to a large extent therefore, a cultural and critical imposition with all that implies. No single romance encapsulates the genre. No single group of romance defines a definite strand, with the possible exception of Arthurian cycles that even then might also indicate 'Matters of Britain'. Instead, texts exceed such categories as easily as they slip into them. Is *Sir Isumbras* family drama, penitential romance, crusade poem or all three? Is *Sir Launfal* most accurately categorized as Arthurian tale or Breton lay, or neither? *Sir Gowther* may be a religious allegory in which Gowther's abject state as a dog re-civilizes this child from hell or may point up key medieval anxieties about dynastic inheritance and the purity of bloodlines. Some romances defy attempts at connection altogether; where to place *The Squire of Low Degree* or *Floris and Blauncheflour*? Others have multiple lines of affinity; ought we to read our only surviving manuscript of *Sir Gawain and the Green Knight*, for example, separate from its numerous Gawain analogues written in English? Or ignore its unusual place in the anonymous Gawain-poet's canon, those allegorical and moralistic poems *Pearl, Patience* and *Cleanness*? Such problems are not unique to medieval romance. As with any work, an individual romance may engender multiple interpretations, often simultaneously. So, too, all texts accrue cultural meanings well beyond their original contexts, some of which will be lost to contemporary audiences. Nevertheless, the especially ambivalent status of medieval romance ensures that, to a large extent, we must read and think about it *differently*. It is to those differences that I turn in the next part of this book.

REVIEW

The material context of romance is highly complex and diffuse, with question marks over

- the provenance of its texts,
- their attribution,
- the conflicted nature of their actual production,
- language issues,
- the physical manifestation of manuscripts and
- their hybrid and intertextual nature.

Equally, the genre exists in tension with many issues pertinent to late medieval society and culture, such as

- an emerging sense of Englishness or nationhood set against foreign expansion, English history (as a colonized nation) and a wider Christian identity,
- social upheaval and changes in economic conditions (influenced by Black Death and war) and
- questions about inheritance and succession.

READING

- For some starting points in considering the difficulties of working with popular tales and their analogues, read the following: Thomas Hahn and Alan Lupack (eds.) (1997), *Retelling Tales*. Cambridge: D.S. Brewer, 1–7; Thomas Hahn (2000), 'Gawain and Popular Chivalric Romance in Britain' in Krueger (ed.), *The Cambridge Companion to Medieval Romance*, 218–34.
- ✳ What is romance 'about'? In what ways might it present difficulties to the modern reader? Read Ad Putter and Jane Gilbert (2000), 'Introduction' in Putter and Gilbert (eds.), *The Spirit of Medieval English Popular Romance*, 1–38.
- Read the following for information on different kinds of medieval romance:
  Barron (2004), 'Arthurian Romance' in Saunders (ed.), *A Companion to Romance*, 65–84; Robert Warm (1999), 'Identity, narrative and participation: defining a context for the Middle English Charlemagne romances' in Field (ed.), *Tradition and Transformation in Medieval Romance*, 87–100; Judith Weiss (2004), 'Insular Beginnings: Anglo-Norman Romance' in Saunders (ed.), *A Companion to Romance from Classical to Contemporary*, 26–44.
- ✳ For basic information about one of the most important elements of medieval romance read: Sarah Kay (2000), Courts, Clerics and Courtly Love' in Krueger (ed.), *The Cambridge Companion to Medieval Romance*, 81–96.

RESEARCH

- How far do you agree that romance is a genre of paradoxes? What kinds of examples support your case?

- What are some of the problems modern readers might face when reading medieval romance and how might we deal with them? How important is it to recreate an 'original' medieval context when we read romances today?
- In what ways might the social changes prompted by Black Death have affected medieval literature, generally, and romance more specifically? Read Rosemary Horrox (ed. and trans.) (1994), *The Black Death*. Manchester: Manchester University Press and think in particular about notions of gender, nationhood and identities. You can find an electronic version of this book on http://books.google.ac.uk
- Find out all that you can about the English 'War of the Roses', Malory's life and the writing of his *Morte DArthur*. Use some of the websites mentioned in the Web Resources section at the end of this book, especially *The Camelot Project*, *Luminarium* and David Wallace's radio documentary to help you.
- Explore the material context of medieval publishing and the impact upon storytelling. Think about issues such as the physical state of existing manuscripts, the impact of visual culture, and manuscript copying and compilation. Starting Points: Sylvia Huot (2000), 'The manuscript context of medieval romance' in Krueger (ed.), *The Cambridge Companion to Medieval Romance*, 60–80; web sites noted in the Web Resources at the end of this book – *NLS Auchinleck MS*, *Vaughan's Auchinleck* and *Medieval Images*.

PART TWO

TEXTS

CHAPTER 3

GENRE AND INTERTEXTUALITY

INTERLACING AND INNOVATION

In the *Morte Darthur*, Malory manipulates a number of French versions of the Arthur legend. On the whole, he remains faithful to these French sources, hence the repetition of tag phrases like 'as the French book says'. He refers to them, in particular, at crisis points in the story in order to add authoritative weight, but also to point up the mythical status of an Arthurian legend he uses as a nostalgic model of 'perfect' Englishness. References increase, therefore, in the closing books when Gareth and his brother are accidentally killed by Lancelot, and Gawain vows vengeance, for example, or when Malory can find no surety in his sources for Arthur's death or possible return.

Yet in many ways Malory takes issue with his French source material to give us an innovative prose romance which is, for many readers, more like a modern novel than a medieval text. He achieves this effect by interlacing stories and episodes in the manner of modern 'soap-drama'. He gathers up the long, rambling threads of the French stories – which work via association and connection to form a vast web-story – in favour of selection, cross-cutting and inter-weaving scenes to give us a briefer, more complete tale. We see this technique in the oral markers that enable him to leave one story and 'Turne we to thys tale' (*Morte DArthur*, 656) or omit the 'grete bookis of sir Launcelot' and all the adventures he had in the French version of 'The Knight of the Cart', claiming to have lost the material (669). Such sleights of hand allow Malory to move to Arthur's death and to stress how Arthur's downfall is a tragic, human drama borne of the failings of a knightly code based on loyalty to the king, and not of the failings of the Holy Grail quest, as in the French Arthurian cycles, or simply of sexual immorality with Guinevere's and Lancelot's adultery, even as the hidden weight of his French reference material leans on his own rendition. Elsewhere, also in 'The Knight of the Cart', he sets the scene, takes us to a castle where we see Guinevere plot to send a child-envoy to Lancelot, then switches to what happens when the child finds him, before alternating between Melegaunt's castle, Lancelot's arrival on the cart, his later imprisonment in the cellar and Arthur's court where they await Lancelot to take up the duel with Melegaunt and save Guinevere from a traitor's death.

For Malory, Arthur's death is the key to his nostalgic vision of 'Englishness'. One of the other ways in which he places this centre stage is by seeding future story-lines or events or using a double-story motif in 'The Knight of the Cart', for example, that allows him to highlight a series of dramatic ironies and, thus, invite retrospective reading. In that same tale, he also manipulates the stock motifs of fairy and romance tales in an effort to draw attention away from sexual impropriety and suggest that Lancelot and Guinevere's love affair was ennobling.

'The Knight of the Cart' opens with a traditional romance motif. It is Maytime, a time of renewal, hope and love when every bud and flower, every heart flourishes (648). This is when lovers call to mind old services and kindnesses forgotten or neglected over the winter. For Malory, though, this is no simple literary device but one which he uses to draw wider parallels. He comments on how green summer is always spoiled by winter's deprivation, before interjecting further to liken this to the ways in which we put aside true love, forget our oaths and loyalties and allow all to become unstable. He says we should allow our hearts to bloom with "vertuouse love" and not behave as lovers do now when love, too quickly granted in the heat of the moment, cools. Before, in "kynge Arthurs dayes" men and women could love each other for years without consummation and stay true, just as Guinevere did: "whyle she lyved she was a trew lover" (649). Here, Malory twists a classic motif to suggest the noble nature of the love triangle at the heart of the Arthurian legend, in contrast to de Troyes' unequivocal depiction of sexual love to which I shall return later in this section.

The incident of 'The Knight of the Cart' begins when Guinevere rides out with her ten special Round Table knights and retinue to do homage to the May. They ride into a wood, typically romance's sign for mischief or transition. Unusually, Lancelot is not with the queen and she is ambushed by Melegaunt who takes advantage of this absence to press his suit to Guinevere. At this point, Malory contrasts Lancelot's devotion of many years standing with Melegaunt's carnal intent (650). In the ensuing battle, Guinevere is forced to go with Melegaunt in order to save the rest of her men, but only if they are allowed to accompany her and remain in the next chamber. In a further twist on familiar romance motifs, they go to Melegaunt's castle, an inverse of its symbolic significance as a civilized, 'safe' space. Guinevere smuggles a ring as a token sign to Lancelot who, of course, rushes to her rescue.

The episode of Melegaunt's abduction of the queen is, in fact, a distorted, contrasting miniature of Lancelot's affair with her. It raises questions about the nature of truth and loyalty and also seeds future events. Melegaunt seeks to dishonour his king's wife and, in so doing, turns on his fellow Round Table knights to attack and kill them. He broadcasts Guinevere's perceived infidelity once he spies the blood-stained sheets. Arthur is forced to respond to these accusations by threatening her life, just as he is obliged to act when rumours become public at the end of the book. Melegaunt almost catches Lancelot in the queen's chamber, just as later they are taken together by Mordred' and Agravant. Guinevere is besieged in a castle, exactly as she is in Joyous Garde later under Lancelot's protection. Melegaunt thinks he has tangible proof of adultery – something Arthur later calls for – with the bloody sheets, even as he accuses Guinevere of behaving exactly as *he* intended to with her. Lancelot accuses him of shaming the queen by walking into her room and approaching her bed, even though he did exactly the same the previous night, albeit at Guinevere's invitation (658). And, of course, Guinevere is defended in this incident by Lancelot, with whom she *has* committed adultery and whose attentions incite the hatred, envy and treason that brings about the collapse of the Round Table, an outcome known to everyone who has ever heard or read the Arthurian legend in whatever shape or form.

GENERIC CONVENTIONS

The poem *Sir Gawain and the Green Knight* is often central to medieval romance study. It survives in a single manuscript alongside *Pearl, Cleanness* and *Patience*. All of these poems are attributed to one anonymous writer known as the Gawain-poet. Most scholars agree that, with the exception of *Sir Gawain and the Green Knight*, these are moral works that raise questions about *Sir Gawain's* meaning and its connection to its companion pieces. Is *Sir Gawain and the Green Knight* a secular, chivalric response to its more spiritual and didactic bedfellows? The poem's Christian allusions are certainly buried within the complex, elusive meanings of symbols like the pentangle on Gawain's shield and the girdle he accepts from the Lady. Its more obvious frame, though, is historical.

Sir Gawain and the Green Knight opens with a familiar romance-chronicle back-story. It tells how Arthur belongs to a line of kings whose antecedents can be traced right back to the fall of Troy and Brutus's subsequent, legendary founding of Britain. This lineage is usually presented as a means of legitimating and, thus, enhancing Arthur's idyllic reign, that distant past through which to critique a contemporaneous medieval world. In *Sir Gawain and the Green Knight*, this convention is used far more ambivalently. The opening lines speak of an unnamed traitor who is responsible for the epic fall of Troy. It is not clear whether this is an implicit reference to the Trojan Antenor who sold out to the Greeks, or to Aeneas whom the poem actually later directly names. In some medieval accounts, it is Aeneas and not Antenor who betrays his nation. If the narrator means Aeneas then the effect of this small detail is far-reaching. The great-grandson of Aeneas is Brutus who allegedly founded Britain. King Arthur is descended from the same lineage with implications for the traditional romance depiction of perfection symbolized by Arthurian Round Table chivalry. This inauspicious legacy might also explain why the Green Knight is able to challenge Arthur and his court in the first place.

Whatever the meaning of this isolated reference, *Sir Gawain and the Green Knight* describes Arthur as the noblest of all the kings of Britain (*Sir Gawain and the Green Knight*, 25–26), even as Britain's history is said to be one of "blysse *and* blunder" (18–19, emphasis mine). The end of the poem returns us to Arthur, Brutus and the city of Troy at exactly the same time as the narrator slips the story into a wider context. He insists that Gawain's tale is but one of a long line of adventures to be read elsewhere in chronicles. Is this an attempt to draw an imaginary generic history for romance or to remind us that romance stories of the kind he recounts here are merely episodes in a wider pattern of woe and misfortune? Or perhaps the remark subsumes secular history, with its see-saw of events, to a heavenly realm of perfection? Maybe the poem's final, and rather unexpected reference, that he who wears the crown of thorns will bring us all to *"blisse"* (2529–30), renders this a Christian poem after all; in which case, perhaps *Sir Gawain and the Green Knight* is best read in conjunction with its manuscript fellows, and not as the stand-alone, master-text of medieval romance, which is how it is often read in contemporary academia. Alternatively, this may simply be a formulaic ending and the story's shifts, between history, legend, Christian story, romance and chronicle, simply part of the hybrid nature of medieval romance whereby a swirl of extra-textual analogues and references continually press on an individual story's meaning.

Romance juxtaposes and interlaces these in ways sometimes hidden to modern audiences. Nevertheless, they are central to how the genre shapes and shifts meaning. *Sir Gawain and the Green Knight*, for instance, is intersected by other tales about Gawain. *The Wedding of Sir Gawain and Dame Ragnell* foregrounds a comic folkore motif, the 'Lothly Lady', to suggest that impeccable private behaviour is more important than public charade, and in so doing bears upon the depiction of courtesy represented in *Sir Gawain and the Green Knight.* So, too, *The Wedding's* emphasis on magic and the old hag of its title cross-cuts the Lady/Morgan-as-crone doubling of *Sir Gawain. Sir Gawain and the Carl of Carlisle,* meanwhile, turns upon the porous divide between monstrous and civilized that structures *Sir Gawain and the Green Knight.*

Perhaps the most famous monster of romance literature is the Green Knight in *Sir Gawain and the Green Knight.* His physique is of gigantic proportions, though it is not entirely clear whether this renders him monstrous or is merely his natural size. The narrator states that he is "Half etayn", a half-giant (*Sir Gawain and the Green Knight,* 140, 723). In addition, he is described as "aghlich", indicating that he is 'fearsome' or 'terrible' (136). Yet there is en element of uncertainty in the Green Knight's depiction that is exacerbated by the fact that his form is always a doubled one. The Green Knight is, of course, actually Bertilak, Gawain's urbane host at Hautdesert. Under Morgan's spell, he is sent to court to frighten Guinevere and cause chaos in the Arthurian kingdom. The early clues to this alternative, enchanted identity only fall into place retrospectively once Bertilak explains everything to Gawain at the end of the poem. Until then, strange details like the Green Knight's colouring mingle with familiar chivalric references to confound even more our grasp of this central figure. The Green Knight is, then, a paradox, an "aghlich mayster [fearsome lord]" (136) carrying a holly branch in one hand as a sign of peace (265–66), and a huge, elaborately decorated weapon, an axe, in the other (208–10, 216–20). The Green Knight may be monstrous but he also clearly belongs to the same aristocratic culture as Gawain and the Camelot courtiers. His dress is fashionable and elaborately trimmed with gold and silk, decorated with birds and butterflies. He wears, too, a cloak edged in white fur (151–67). Though he bears an axe, the rest of his armour has been left at home, or so he claims in his opening speeches; he is certainly dressed as a knight at leisure would be. This, together with Bertilak's courtesy at Hautdesert further reminds us that he is inextricably linked to the same knightly code as Gawain.

Equally, the exaggerated description of the Carl in *Sir Gawain and the Carl of Carlisle* enhances that of the Green Knight by virtue of its proximity to its 'sibling' poem. The Carl's physical appearance matches conventional depictions of the giant in late medieval romance. He is broad with coarse features, and of enormous height and power with thick arms and legs like a bear. He has a huge mouth to denote his appetitive nature. Savage beasts roam loose next to him around the fireside: a wild bull, a fierce boar, a lion and a massive bear. These are his "whelpys four", monstrous versions of the domestic dog companions common in chivalric households (*Sir Gawain and the Carl of Carlisle*, 247–50, quote 235). The Carl is a more immediate and obvious threat than the Green Knight, an adversarial figure rather than a puzzling one. Nevertheless, both his appearance and his behaviour intensify the *potential* for chaos in *Sir Gawain and the Green Knight*.

The Carl's home – its name and setting are the clues – inverts Arthur's Camelot. Similarly, when Gawain and his companions seek refuge in the Carl's castle, the porter expresses sorrow and warns of their host's reputation (*Sir Gawain and the Carl of Carlisle*, 196, 209–10) to echo the words of Gawain's guide to the Green Chapel who tries to encourage him to abandon his quest (2118–25). The 'Exchange of Blows' in the *Carl of Carlisle* is literal rather than symbolic as it is in *Sir Gawain*. Bishop Baldwyn and Sir Kay both fail the Carl's secret hospitality test when they chase off his foal; one is struck on the head and the other in the eye (*Sir Gawain and the Carl of Carlisle*, 302–30). In contrast, and with obvious allusion to *Sir Gawain and the Green Knight*, Gawain must prove his worth by hurling a spear into his host's face and trusting it will not harm him. Later he is shamed when the Carl recognizes his desire for his beautiful wife. He then has to make love to her while the Carl looks on and desist when instructed to do so (*Sir Gawain and the Carl of Carlisle*, 439–95). The Carl thus reminds us of what might happen if order breaks down. Somewhere within him, though, is a hint of redemptive courtliness: the animals in his isolated, ill-reputed castle sit near the hearth, which symbolizes civilized society; a magic foal lurks on the edges, exposed and vulnerable until Gawain brings it safely inside. Such details suggest how easily thresholds might be crossed. 'Outside' can creep in and erode the values of 'inside', or, equally, the monster might be tamed. Either way, simply to expel everything that is undesirable is no guarantee that it will disappear. *Sir Gawain and the Carl of Carlisle*'s humorous replication of many of the events and motifs of *Sir Gawain* also calls attention to the ways in which identities are constructed and demand repeated performance if they are to embed as natural or given. The poem also parallels how desire must be regulated within a structuring heterosexual paradigm that can never fully conceal the illicit possibilities it seeks to expel, something amply demonstrated in the explicit, homo-erotic voyeurism of the bedroom scene in *The Carl of Carlisle*. The episode has especial resonance for the more covert triangular relationships of *Sir Gawain and the Green Knight*.

Many of the texts explored in Part Two of this volume are equally buffeted by other stories and genres. A large number of the poems I have selected are what is known as Breton lays, an identification that poses several problems. In their introduction to their collection of primary Breton lay texts, Laskaya and Salisbury argue that these romances comprise a special group and ought, therefore, to be read as such (Laskaya and Salisbury, 2001: 1–12). The pair acknowledges the difficulties of classifying the lays which at their simplest level are merely story versions of poems sung by Bretons to a musical accompaniment. Equally the genre – if that is what it is – is shadowed and partially defined by Marie de France's collection of twelve lays, even though she was probably writing in England, not the Breton region. The poems certainly seem to have been composed at around the same time, somewhere between 1150 and 1450. Most are set in Brittany, Normandy or Wales and exhibit features of oral performance as befits their roots in minstrelsy but so do many other romances. Most foreground love and many have elements of faery. This appears to be part of a tradition of magic that allegedly transferred to Brittany from Britain when the ancient Celts fled there in the fifth century. Equally, there are differences in dialect, metre and rhyme, again as with other romances of the time.

In spite of this, Laskaya and Salisbury argue that to read the lays as part of a wider romance genre misses nuances and the import of issues unique to Breton lays (Laskaya and Salisbury, 2001: vii). Yet, in many respects, the nuances they speak of are part of a larger swirl of hidden stories and back-drops that contribute to the fluidity of romance as a whole. This, in my view, negates the need to sub-classify them. If anything at all is specific to the Breton lay, it is perhaps its particular shape-shifting literary history. Breton lays are not merely stories told by medieval Bretons living in a particular region of France. They are also old stories belonging to a tradition that came from Britain out of a distant past. As such, Laskaya and Salisbury's observation that Brutus and Breton "share the same genealogy and cultural heritage" is possibly more significant than attempts to sub-classify them. This shared past, when put together with English claims on Breton during the Hundred Years War (1337–1453), is perhaps why English vernacular lays were so popular in late medieval England; they were co-opted as part of a cultural, even political, agenda for "reinstating a . . . heritage" (Laskaya and Salisbury, 2001: 7) as well as speaking to social and familial concerns made especially pertinent in the light of Black Death. For now, I wish to note first the controversy surrounding the lays' classification, and, second, the ways in which, like other romances, they are often hybrid as opposed to pure forms with all the ambivalences of meaning that attend in these generically indeterminate instances.

Emaré, Chaucer's the *Man of Law's Tale* in *The Canterbury Tales*, and 'The Tale of Constance' in John Gower's moral work *Confessio Amantis*, are all versions of a conventional folklore and romance 'Accursed Queens' saga in which an eminent woman is exiled and cast adrift in a boat. The story's impetus is usually incest; this is certainly the case in *Emaré*, but not, or at least not directly, so in Chaucer's account. The rudderless boat in which the protagonist drifts is variously an image of faith or the Ship of the Church in Christian iconography. In folkore it is more commonly the means by which the souls of the dead are transported to the other side. The tale often mingles romance, folktale, Christian myth or hagiography (saints' lives). It is also found in history, most notably in Nicholas Trevet's *Anglo-Norman*

Chronicle where it is the birth story of the real-life Emperor Mauricius of Rome and an account of his mother Constance's attempt to spread Christianity throughout Europe. In this respect, Emaré and Custance (the figure in the *Man of Law's Tale*) might be said to represent female sacrifice, exemplary virtue and saintly constancy in the face of adversity. A reading that emphasizes such model femininity is supported by this mixing of sources and genres.

Sir Gowther combines Breton lay, folklore, penitential romance, saint's life and family drama to evoke a number of simultaneous readings and, once again, demonstrate the porous nature of romance as a genre. In one sense, *Gowther* is typical folktale where the central character might be read as a 'Wish Child' born of a monstrous or demonic father. These fathers inhabit woods or wild places, spots that like the half-human, highly sexual, aggressive 'madmen' or 'wodwos' who live in them teeter on the edges of civilization (Middle English 'wode' means both 'wood' and 'mad'). Frequently they are depicted engaging in all the usual pursuits of chivalry before going on to commit atrocity. Gowther's father appears first in an orchard in the guise of his mother's husband before having sex with his mother (raping her?) and reverting to his demonic state as a hairy fiend. He bequeaths some of these attributes to Gowther who, in the first half of the story, rampages throughout the land to rape, murder, pillage and commit arson.

The wild men of folklore often intersect literary depictions of Merlin to whom Gowther is explicitly related in the tale (*Sir Gowther*, 97–99). Medieval audiences would recognize Merlin from the Arthurian cycles and other works. In these he appears in a number of guises: as hybrid-monster, as an Antichrist figure who will, according to the biblical Book of Revelations, end the world, and also more positively as a magician-cum-prophet and Arthur's mentor. The 'Wish Child' motif also has dual valency paralleling biblical stories like those of St. Anne, mother of the Virgin Mary. Here, after a long and barren marriage, someone prays for a child. An angel then announces the impending birth of a special baby to grant the parent their wish. Gowther's mother wishes in exactly that way and even invents an angelic visitation to ensure he is passed off as her husband's (50–66, 83–93). Saints' lives similarly rework the motif of the Wild Man to offer a holy man in twisted form. In these tales, the Wild Man's monstrous body symbolizes his sin and his exiled state represents penance. These wild holy men inhabit wildernesses or deserts, wear animal skins and live alone in abject states – sometimes as beggars or fools – reminiscent of the desert-father saints of hagiography. In this way, then, the influence of other versions in other genres bears on this story to ensure Gowther's origins are demonic and saintly at one and the same time.

Sir Gowther weaves Christian allusions into its typical romance, family-drama story. As part of his rehabilitation, and to atone for former misdeeds, he lives as a dog under the table in the second half of the story. At the end he becomes "Goddus child" (673), confesses, learns how to pray and receive forgiveness, and is lord of all Christian knights (713). He is actively spiritual, described as charitable, obedient, pious and loved by all the Christian folk who hated him before (727–28), while the closing verses repeatedly stress how he receives God's grace (715–56). In short, Gowther redeems all those antireligious acts of his early life – the raped nuns and torched convent, the clerics he murdered, the hermits he set fire to, and all the masses and sermons he refused to attend (168–204).

CHIVALRY

It is almost impossible to explore medieval romance without first considering the complex nature of those chivalric communities upon which so many of its stories are based. The exemplary court is almost always Arthurian, if not in actuality then in effect. Arthurian fellowship often stands for perfection. As a story of origins, King Arthur's lineage, traced back to Brutus and the founding of Britain, might represent a glorious, distant past through which to carve a future. The Round Table fellowship Arthur establishes foregrounds the inviolability of oaths and promises of allegiance, first to king and then to each other, and so models a similar founding principle or ideal for contemporaneous medieval society. Chivalry is held together by knightly kinship. A man might prove himself a worthy fellow knight in a number of ways but, ultimately, he had to satisfy the demands of bravery and physical prowess as a warrior, courtesy, fellowship, compassion and fidelity or 'trouthe'. Chivalry also has a spiritual or moral dimension whereby a knight should trust in God's protection (hence the knights of the Crusades or the infamous Templar knights fighting Islam) and act in a virtuous, exemplary manner at all times. Courtesy is a particularly conflicted attribute that incorporates a number of different features: hospitality, name or reputation, upholding truth and not breaking vows ('trowthe'). Courtesy also demands politeness in the sense of formality of speech and manners – which includes gallant devotion to women – or adherence to set rules and behaviours. Courtesy also often has a moral dimension.

In many respects, chivalry is a literary rather than an actual ideal or convention. Its feudal roots probably relegate it to a distant, outmoded past, as I stated in Part One. As such, romances often employ it as a nostalgic ideal through which to refract and critique medieval culture or contemporaneous concerns. Above all, because it functions, theoretically at least, as a masculine symbol of order or restraint, chivalry frequently becomes a space in which to play out the faultlines of its corresponding masculine 'symbolic' or real world. Equally, chivalry's stress on externals, its public, often theatrical, displays sometimes evoke a gap between outside, surface appearance and the inner, more affective (emotional) leanings of the knight it produces. This clash between personal integrity and a complete, fully articulated, masculine subject is something to which I shall return in more extended discussions of selected romance texts.

The chivalric world is pulled together by homosocial bonds: that is, it is effected and sustained by the fraternity of knights which comprises its 'family'. Personal kinship – whether literal or through obligation to others – knits it up, and public actions cement it. This is then repeated across different romance stories to give it a literary force or resonance that possibly chivalry never had in real life. The long list of names at the start of *Sir Gawain and the Carl of Carlisle* – Gawain, Perceval, Sir Kay, Ywain, Lancelot, Lanval and a host of others – conjure a glorious Arthurian family (25–66) replicated in other tales like Malory's *Morte Darthur*. Kinship is also central to the plot of *The Wedding of Sir Gawain and Dame Ragnell*. The monster-man Sir Gromer Somer Jour threatens to kill Arthur when he thinks Arthur has given his own nephew, Gawain, lands that he believes are his by right. In order to avoid death, Arthur must discover what women most desire, a quest in which he is aided by Gawain. When the 'Lothly Lady' Dame Ragnell supplies the answer, her reward is to demand marriage with Gawain. He accedes, even though she is a fiend – because he is obligated to Arthur by virtue as kin and also as one of his Round Table knights. Marriage to Ragnell thus reinforces chivalric bonds, as well as enhancing Gawain's reputation as a model of courtesy. When the monstrous Dame Ragnell asks Gawain to kiss her on their wedding night, he says he will do more, and freely turns to her. This exemplary behaviour breaks the spell of enchantment which she is under. Ragnell is revealed as the beautiful sister of Sir Gromer and becomes the woman that Gawain loved the most of all his wives. Though she dies within five years of their marriage, the pair has a son, Guinglain, who becomes another well-reputed Round Table knight (*The Wedding of Sir Gawain and Dame Ragnell*, 805–35). These complex affiliations, some of them superfluous to the plot, amply demonstrate the importance of allegiance and kinship in an exemplary chivalric model.

Other romances highlight how chivalry – and, by implication, all culture – constructs itself through a series of public displays or reiterated performances. The gap between public and private behaviour is perhaps never wider than it appears in the popular romance *Sir Launfal*. The opening litany of Round Table knights, together with the telling detail that Launfal has stewarded the court for ten successful years, seemingly secure it as a principle of masculine order. Everyone has a recognized place until the arrival of Guinevere. Arthur's queen is spotlighted as pivotal to subsequent disruption from the start (*Sir Launfal*, 44–48). Guinevere's public insult to Launfal (67–72) prompts his long estrangement from chivalric society during which he becomes invisible to it. Launfal is increasingly shunned by society as the physical trappings of his former knightly status literally fall away from him. His robes are torn, he has no money or equipment, not even shoes to go to church in or tack for his horse (190–210). When he begs his companion knights, Hugh and John, Arthur's nephews, to conceal the extent of his penury from the court, he underscores the importance of public exhibition (142–47). Despite Guinevere's attempt to extract malicious gossip from them, the knights keep their word, and even praise Launfal to uphold chivalric kinship (157–68, 177–80). Similarly, once Launfal is restored to that world, all those who previously scorned him now vie for his attention. Tryamour re-equips him and promises him eternal life and safety in battle (315–65), Launfal wins several tournaments to restore his good name. Arthur recalls him to court and restores his stewardship, as well as celebrating him at a feast. We are reminded of how everyone likes and esteems him (639–45). Even Guinevere pursues him once she realizes the extent of his reputation (649–54).

The public restoration of chivalric fraternity comes, however, at the expense of private, moral worth. This crucial mismatch blows apart any notion of intrinsic virtue and exposes chivalry as a sham.

Launfal's notoriety is bought with the secret help of Tryamour. His own knightly prowess is not enough against the fearsome Sir Valentine who has come to test Launfal's name and he experiences "moche shame" (578) as he loses ground. Victory comes only with magic help (577–94). Later, stung by Guinevere's taunts about his masculinity, Launfal disavows his promise to Tryamour – and to chivalry's demands to protect ladies – and reveals her existence. Along the way, he insults Arthur's queen (691–99). Suddenly personal standards of behaviour fall far short of the external man.

A chivalric order that cannot also stand up to public scrutiny is, of course, profoundly compromised. In practice, the situation is far more complex than this. Arthur has no choice but to take his wife's word over that of even his most loyal knight, one who has twice proved that his name is good (775–77). Launfal's fellow knights know of Guinevere's rumoured ill-repute and so can undoubtedly estimate the likely truth of her assertions, yet cannot speak their fears in open court. Allegiance to Arthur and to the chivalry he embodies means that they must somehow evade the issue of 'trawthe' upon which everything rests, even as it is now at stake. Accordingly, they advise Launfal to produce the lover of whom he boasted and, when he cannot, advocate exile rather than the traitor's death his crime deserves (835–46). In a parallel manoeuvre, Launfal loses integrity the moment he accepts Tryamour's advances and then later talks about her (see 315–65). Here romance's familiar 'Lothly Lady' motif, which taps into chivalry's insistence on external show, is inverted to exacerbate anxieties about public conduct. Just as the court must hide the secret of Guinevere's likely adultery so order can prevail, Launfal must never publicly acknowledge Tryamour, especially when the revelation is prompted by petty revenge (691–99). At the end of the story, Launfal follows Tryamour into faery. His voluntary absence speaks to the failures of a chivalry so predicated on outward signs that in the end it can offer no more than an illusory satisfaction. This vanishing act shows, too, how symbols shift according to the perspectives of those who perpetrate or invoke them and allow silences to undermine public, professed scripts and norms.

SIGNS AND SYMBOLS

One of the principle identifying features of medieval romance is its complex use of symbols. These range from details of clothing or armour, chivalric objects such as an engraved cup or a magical pair of gloves, and on to significant colours, numbers or shapes like the pentangle depicted on Gawain's shield in *Sir Gawain and the Green Knight*. Symbolic meaning accrues both from specific textual contexts *and* through the circulation of similar objects or motifs across many different tales. As such, medieval audiences came to recognize – and take pleasure in – the immediate power of certain, sometimes apparently minor, details of a story. Those same motifs worked as shorthand for writers as well as a base point from which they might subvert an audience's expectations or subtly alter meaning, perhaps by signalling several cues at once.

In this way, too, romance's symbols allow the genre to become self-referential so that certain echoes even carry through to its contemporary consumers (see Part Three). So, cups, swords, cloaks and rings are exchange and/or recognition tokens while some trees or entry into a forest or wilderness often flips a story and its protagonist into another dimension. Baby Freine is abandoned wearing a beautiful cloak through which her mother will later reclaim her in *Lay le Freine*. Blaunicheflour is exchanged for a magnificent cup which Floris uses to barter his way into the harem where the Emir holds her prisoner in *Floris and Blauncheflour*. A broken sword and faery gloves enable Degaré to recognize his parents (*Sir Degaré*). Herodis falls asleep under a tree from where she is abducted into the land of faery in *Sir Orfeo*. Trees or forests frequently mark the borders of other worlds in romance and always signal danger. In *Sir Orfeo*, the "ympe-tree" is an unnatural, grafted tree in contrast to the free-growing wood of which it is part. It both spirits Herodis away and also cues her return; when Orfeo sees her in the underworld, she sits in suspended animation beneath the same tree (*Sir Orfeo*, 363–84). Similarly, in *Sir Launfal*, Launfal reclines in the shade of a tree from where he is taken to meet his faery lover Tryamour. Degaré's mother conceives him when she wanders through a forest while the rest of her retinue sleep beneath a chestnut tree. The tree both maps the edge of the real and – according to Christian iconography where it symbolizes chastity – flags the purity of a lineage perpetuated through her son. The heroine of *Lay le Freine* takes her name from the ash tree in which she is found, while her sister is le Codre meaning 'hazel'. Their names stem from Celtic myth and so shift the pair out of real-time signification into a distant and, therefore, safe space through which to explore medieval contemporaneous issues. The ash was also said to have magical, healing properties to protect against witchcraft and be unable to bear fruit. These symbols interlace to suggest the ways in which women – here sisters and mothers – are separated and effaced in masculine-dominated society, even as they hold it together by 'bearing fruit' or replicating family connections.

Meaning is, however, never singular in romance, and so even familiar or recurrent symbols work differently in individual stories. His mother, the queen, gives Floris a ring in *Floris and Blauncheflour* to safeguard him on his travels. At the end of the tale, Floris tries to pass it on to Blauncheflour when the Emir threatens murder as he discovers them in bed together. She insists that Floris must keep it and so spotlights a mutual devotion that incites the Emir's compassion. Here the ring has no magical properties after all but exerts a different kind of charm, that of love. Elsewhere in the same poem a ring functions as an identification emblem; the innkeeper gives one to Floris to show to the bridgekeeper from whom he will receive hospitality and access (*Floris and Blauncheflour*, 505–10).

Both instances employ the rings as part of a wider transaction of reputation and renown that also parallels the story's main symbol, that of the engraved cup. Floris's parents sell his beloved Blauncheflour to a group of merchants in return for a marvellous cup. The parents then pass the cup to Floris in recognition of its material value and as an aid to him in his quest to find Blauncheflour. We are told that there is nothing else like it in the world, yet its story is far from unique. The cup is illustrated with the abduction of Helen by Paris, which sparked the Trojan war. Here, though, the act is recounted as a tale of mutual love, like that of Floris and Blauncheflour. The engravings also tell how the Trojan Aeneas won the cup and took it to Lombardy where he gave it to his paramour. In one sense, then, the cup is a love token. Later, though, we learn that it fell into the hands of Caesar from whom it was subsequently stolen by one of the merchants who exchanged it for Blauncheflour. That same merchant-thief is happy to trade it for he recognizes that Blauncheflour is worth not one but three cups like this (163–85, 191–200). The merchants later sell Blauncheflour on to the Emir as a handmaiden in his harem for seven times her body weight (196–97).

The cup is thus invested with several meanings at once. It is a love token *and* a precious object of exchange, meanings that immediately conflate ideas about the commodification of women. Its 'history' is steeped in trade and its material worth measured both by its obvious

51

beauty and battles over its ownership – just as Blauncheflour (and Helen) are also regarded as prizes. Equally, its lineage is one of loss and separation. Floris, Blauncheflour, Helen and Aeneas are all forced to leave their homes, whether by virtue of a quest, slavery, abduction or exile. Such estrangements slip its owners or subjects into a passive, feminized position which, in turn, has implications for Floris's journey. Though Floris is often indistinguishable from Blauncheflour, his journey is, in part, a symbolic quest to claim adult, masculine identity. Unlike other romances which are punctuated by battles with monsters, Floris's voyage involves 'feminine' trickery and slippery manoeuvre. Cups function as bartering tools through which he penetrates spaces and gets ever closer to his beloved. Twice Floris tries to exchange a cup (and gold) for news of Blauncheflour's where-abouts (417–24, 475–80). The bridgekeeper too tells him to wager a cup on a game of chess to ensure he gets past those who guard the Emir's harem (671–704).

Conflicted symbols

Tournaments are a popular plot device and symbolic motif in medi-eval romance. They test both knight and masculinity and are part of the theatre of chivalry in which everything turns on an external display meant to match inner virtue. As such, many romances blur a public–private demarcation in order to intensify moral worth and, so, have their protagonists conceal identity or battle it out over several days. *Sir Gowther* combines both to stage a three-day tourna-ment in its second half when Gowther is trying to redeem himself. He fights each day in different coloured armour, having earlier prayed for chivalric implements, (armour, horse, shield) secretly pro-vided by his lord's mute daughter. Each time he wins before return-ing to his abject state as a dog beneath the table. On the third, he is injured and the daughter falls from a tower. She lies in a coma for three days – to match the length of Gowther's rehabilitation in the jousting – before she awakens, and, with her voice restored, identifies Gowther as their family's disguised champion.

The tournament, thus, marks a process of recovery for both Gowther and the girl. Their marriage at the end signifies their re-entry into the 'real' social world of culture and language. She names him as their saviour and he takes up his proper place as a knight. Each of the three days marks another stage of a process that is part of an inbuilt, spiritual ideal of perfection. Gowther fights first in black, then red, and finally white to reflect his successful penance. The symbolism of *Sir Gowther's* tournament is part Christian but also has more worldly chivalric connotations in a manner familiar to romance audiences. These feed too into the significance of the dogs in the tale. A silent, penitent Gowther co-habits with the dogs that sit beneath his lord's table in the great hall at the heart of the castle. These are ordinary spaniels or hunting dogs, often depicted in medieval iconography as obedient, faithful companions to humans. Like the dogs, Gowther is domesticated; he learns compliance and restraint, qualities he lacked in the first half of his life as a demon, a wild, animalistic usurper of civilized codes. His state in the castle as an unclean beast is necessary if he is to atone for his past. Also present are greyhounds. These creatures pass him scraps of food from mouths cleaned by the lord's daughter. Greyhounds were thought to combine aristocratic merit and spiritual refinement. Like Gowther – and their 'mistress' – they were thought to be mute, rarely barking. They symbolize purity, cleanness and control.

Chivalric combat features, too, in *Sir Degaré* as part of a maturational quest in which he must uncover his birth story before he can take his place in the world. Two symbols work in conjunction with each other as part of the way in which Degaré achieves his gendered (masculine), chivalric identity. Degaré's faery-father leaves a broken sword with his mother after he has raped her, with instructions to give it to their son and tell him to come and find him. Degaré's father keeps the sword's broken-off tip in a pouch, waiting for his son to reclaim it (*Sir Degaré*, 119–31). When, later, the two unwittingly fight each other, his father recognizes the sword and the pair, at last, meet (1048–62).

At first glance, the sword is a simple recognition sign but it also has significance for Degaré's wider identity in the world – not just as a 'son' but as a masculine subject. A commonplace of psychoanalysis is that we achieve subjectivity (identity in its broadest terms) by enacting a family drama symbolized in the myth of Oedipus. Oedipus accidentally kills his father and unknowingly marries his mother with devastating personal and social consequences. Freud expanded on this to identify the moment at which boys challenge their fathers in a metaphorical battle to gain the phallus (language and privilege) and so step into the world as fully-fledged masculine subjects: that is rational, controlled and in charge of language and culture. In this sense, the damaged sword indicates Degaré's incomplete, in-progress identity. His mother claims to know nothing of his father save the story of the sword he left behind (702). Its tip was lost during his own fight for maturity when he killed a giant (symbolic and distorted father-figure) by hitting it so hard on its head with the sword that the point snapped off (119–31). Degaré's mother repeats what his father said: he must take it if he "were a man" (706). Degaré reiterates the idea that the sword represents masculinity when he takes it from its scabbard and, remarking on its weight and strength, declares that whoever owns it then "he was a man" (707–12).

Questions about paternity and masculinity are, of course, only one side of this family drama. A Freudian model of psychoanalysis also tells how a child must separate from its blissful unity with the mother and accept the domination of the father with 'his' masculine laws, culture and language. Forever after, we desire and seek to recapture what we have lost. Boys might later recover that maternal loss, in part at least, in a heterosexual relationship; hence, most romances end with a marriage. *Sir Degaré* sidesteps the somewhat reductive simplicity of this paradigm, however, and, instead, confronts the disturbing nature of desire through the symbol of his mother's gloves. When Degaré's mother abandons him, she leaves for him not just his father's sword but a pair of gloves he sent to her from the world of faery. These, she writes in the letter telling of his birth, will be how he will recognize his one true love, for they will fit no other. Yet this simple recognition sign becomes something far more ambivalent than a love token passed from father to mother, Degaré to lover. These are feminized objects associated with 'outside', the realm of magic, and with repressed desire (the rape leading to Degaré's conception). They are also tokens by which all that is other might successfully enter, and, through marriage, order the real world. They are at once a recognition token *and* part of Degaré's birth story, which is why his mother leaves them in the cradle, together with the broken sword and instructions for beginning to piece together his identity. The most disturbing aspect of these gloves is the repeated realization that they will only fit not just Degaré's future wife but no human hands except those of the mother who bears him (194–99). Thus audiences are set up for the moment when Degaré marries his own mother, for she alone is the woman who satisfies both criteria (213–18, 311–16).

The illicit sexual desires invested in these gloves – rape and possible incest – mark them as a potential symbol of disruption. They are alluring and erotic, a feminized symbol. At the same time, the gloves have the power to rectify this family's dysfunction by correctly identifying, first, Degaré's mother, and, second, his proper bride. In this sense, they bear a dual valency, functioning also as a token of order, and, hence, seemingly masculine. The gloves confer proper names and roles. When Degaré unwittingly marries his mother, the king makes him his heir; in other words, his grandfather confers legitimacy on his own grandson, albeit unknowingly. Disaster still looms, though, in the shape of an incestuous consummation averted only when Degaré suddenly recalls that he ought to test his new bride's suitability by asking her to try on the gloves. His mother immediately realizes the situation. She tries them on to declare herself not his wife but his mother (665–70). The gloves are the means by which the plot might progress. Public acknowledgement of maternity precedes the final part of his quest, which will involve him finding both his father and his proper wife. The ambivalence of the gloves is a crucial counterpoint to the sword. Both are necessary if Degaré is to achieve full subjectivity.

In *Sir Gawain and the Green Knight* the colour of Gawain's adversary is one of several symbols that bear upon the poem's meaning. The monstrous Yuletide intruder who challenges Arthurian order is coloured green, as is his horse. The knight's hair, beard, and complexion all have a verdant hue to flag, in the first instance, his status as one outside the rules of the chivalric community. In medieval iconography green is often associated, too, with traitors; here the Green Knight threatens King Arthur himself and seeks to up-end notions of chivalry. The colour is also allied with nature, a symbolism strengthened by comparing his beard to a bush (*Sir Gawain and the Green Knight*, 182) and having the Green Knight carry an evergreen holly branch (207), representing, in part, eternal life. Later on in the story Gawain must meet the Green Knight at the Green Chapel, which turns out to be an enclosed and rocky natural feature of the landscape. These signs link the Green Knight with nature, the civilized court's polar opposite, even if his role as instigator of, and deadly opponent in, the 'Exchange of Blows' will always be more dramatic than actual for he represents natural life, rather than death.

So, too, the symbolism of the pentangle depicted on Gawain's shield provokes a range of, sometimes contradictory, readings. The lengthy description of Gawain's arming in is a traditional feature of romance and part of a number of rituals – armouring, feasting, games or tournaments, hospitality rites – that serve to reinforce chivalric codes. Chivalry turns upon outward sign and symbol. It is a theatrical display of valour, wealth and courtesy that enhances chivalry's strength as a community. At the same time, emphasis upon visual or spectacular moments might equally highlight the inherent emptiness of its traditions in a medieval world rapidly discarding old, feudal affiliations.

At first, the description of the preparations for Gawain's journey to meet the Green Knight, as he promised, seem straightforward. The ceremony of Gawain's arming, its ritualistic piece-by-piece action, together with the opulence of his own and his horse's dress, indicates his great prestige (566–618). He is both Arthur's nephew and the only knight of the Round Table prepared to take up the Green Knight's challenge. Gawain's shield is brought to him towards the end of this arming scene (619–22). As might be expected, it is decorated in Gawain's heraldic colours of red and gold, features which identify the prestige of his family name. It also has a pentangle painted upon it, a five-sided figure, which is repeated on his surcoat (637). This emblem is unique to the story, found nowhere else in either romance or records of heraldic signs. It is, then, clearly a crucial symbol.

The pentangle's meaning is the subject of both critical controversy and some confusion in the narrative. The narrator's explanation of it is long and difficult to follow. To begin with, he defines it as a sign of "trawthe" [truth] established through king Solomon (625–66). Solomon's significance for medieval audiences was particularly conflicted. He was variously represented as one of the greatest and wisest spiritual authorities of all time, as a sexual sinner led astray by women, and as a founder of black magic arts. Already, then, the pentangle's meaning is neither singular nor clear. The narrator also claims that ordinary people know it as "the endless knot" (630, 662). Its context is, thus, framed as simultaneously learned and popular. The fact that it is endless or unbroken in form imputes it with the quality of wholeness. Medieval writers, iconographers and theologians regarded wholeness as a sign of moral worth and spiritual perfection. Proper bodies – that is to say institutions like royalty and the law, as well as actual, individual bodies – were always complete, an attribute regarded as masculine (though, of course, some iconic bodies – Christ's body – were also feminine and ruptured). The idea of the pentangle as an endless knot signs Gawain as potentially virtuous. It underscores, too, a masculine identity that is made visually apparent by the armour which covers him from head to toe. Other details corroborate the suggestion that the knot is a suitable image for Gawain. He is said to be faithful in five ways and five times each way (632) to match its five points. He is faultless in terms of his physical prowess, a crucial aspect of knighthood, and also in his five senses and five fingers (640–41) with a powerful, manly grip. Another set of five lists the moral qualities which chivalric society esteemed. These are franchise, fellowship, cleanness, courtesy and pity or piety; Gawain has them all. He is also spiritually sound for he trusts in the five wounds of Christ, or so the narrator says, and the five joys of the Virgin Mary (640–47).

All of these values are interdependent, just like the five, endless sides of the pentangle. The narrator implies that without any one of its features the pentangle will unravel. Similarly, Gawain must not fail in any single aspect of the 'truth' the pentangle ostensibly represents (656–61). Yet the pentangle's significance remains ambiguous. One meaning is as a sign of the perfect, Christian knight looking to Christ and Mary for salvation; in which case, Gawain's truth becomes 'faith' or the absolute truth of God. Another meaning turns on notions of moral truth or personal integrity. It also points to a public or social identity as a perfect knight of the Round Table, even as it takes in sexual weakness through its association with King Solomon. Is Christian faith subsumed to chivalry or the other way round? Is faith – or social identity – off-set by the connection between Solomon the black magic master and those other hints of magic that propel the plot? The pentangle is eternal or endless, yet never quite symbolizes perfection or unity. Equally, the fact that the shield is "happed" or "fettled" [fastened] on to Gawain (655–56) suggests its virtues are somehow external to the man (like the rest of his armour) and not part of his intrinsic nature. In the same way, Gawain is said to be "enourned" or adorned with its virtues (634).

Thus the story's events may be read as demonstrating a gap between the different components of a chivalric code and the inner man. Such a suggestion is supported by the passage in the final fit where Gawain dresses for his encounter in the Green Chapel (2026–29). Earlier, as he leaves Arthur's court, Gawain's shield and pentangle are both fully described. By the close of the poem, it is more vaguely noted in the phrase "the conysaunce of the clere workes" (2026), as something no longer full of "trawthe" but simply another emblem embroidered on his surcoat. When Gawain finally returns to the court, the narrator makes no mention at all of the pentangle. Instead, Gawain's chivalric and personal sign now is another equally ambiguous item, the girdle which he wears as a baldric.

What are we to make of this slippery and shifting symbolism? Perhaps it speaks of the failures of chivalry or tells something of the covert and multiple ways in which we construct social worlds. Maybe the pentangle evokes some of the challenges to the Christian Church in medieval times. Or is it an external symbol of masculinity – itself problematic – pinned on to the as-yet untried Gawain and concealing something far more conflicted beneath? Possibly it has no singular truth at all but enacts some, or even all, of these possibilities at once.

The girdle

Above all, the symbols in *Sir Gawain and the Green Knight* interlace, and cross-cut, to operate both independently of each other, and in contiguity as part of a wider indeterminacy at work in the poem. One example of this is the meaning of the girdle, which the Lady gives to Gawain. Up to that point, Gawain has courteously resisted all of her attempts to flatter and seduce him. He turns down the offer of her body, as well as the gift of a gold ring (1817–22) because, having brought nothing of value with him, he cannot engage the rules of hospitality and match it (1808–09, 1836–38). Initially he rejects, too, the Lady's gift of her girdle. The ground shifts once she tells him that the girdle has magical properties, which protect its wearer from death. The narrator of the poem has already detailed how the forthcoming encounter with the Green Knight in the Green Chapel weighs on Gawain's mind. In one portentous moment, Gawain chooses to accept the girdle after all.

We are told that he takes it as a "sleight" (1858); that is, as a magic talisman and nothing more. He agrees to keep the gift a secret for the Lady's sake when she does not wish her husband Bertilak to know (1863). Gawain hides the girdle, not even mentioning it when he goes to confession (1870–82), either because he perceives it as trivial (unlikely) or because he is immediately caught up in the web of lies and concealment its ownership seems to provoke. By hiding it from Bertilak, Gawain compromises chivalric honour. On the one hand, as befits his 'truth' as a knight, he behaves gallantly towards the Lady by protecting her reputation. On the other, he breaks his vow to a fellow knight by failing to declare it in accordance with the 'Exchange of Winnings' pact he made with Bertilak, his host at Hautdesert. Bertilak presents a fox pelt as the spoil of his day's hunting. Gawain ought, in turn, to produce the girdle and does not. This failure of truth is exacerbated by Gawain's later contrasting response to the guide who accompanies him to the Green Chapel. The guide remarks that if Gawain fled at this moment, none would think the worse of him for it is a hellish place. Above all, the guide promises he would keep such an action a secret between him and Gawain. Gawain responds with displeasure. In his reply, he insists on honour and the high standards of chivalry, even though his actions – he is wearing the girdle beneath his armour – are at odds with his speech (2126–35).

At one level, then, the girdle is a key plot device that precipitates a series of events, leading to the climax of the poem. Equally, it intersects a range of ideas and themes integral to the story. One of these is the way the girdle functions as an integer of chivalry. Gawain's ownership of it compromises honour, personal integrity and a chivalric 'trouthe' flagged elsewhere by, for instance, the sign of the pentangle. The manner in which Gawain dresses for his encounter in the Green Chapel intensifies these meanings. The Lady warns him to fasten the girdle tight in order to enhance its protective magic (1851–54). Gawain winds it twice around his waist, over the belt holding his sword in place. At this point, the narrator intervenes to declare that Gawain wears the girdle for its supernatural powers, not because it is beautiful (2037–42).

At precisely the same point in the narrative, the girdle is also described as a "drurye", meaning love token (2032–34). Gawain handles the item as though it is a gift of love. The text calls attention to the lovely appearance of the girdle and the surcoat. The pentangle is no longer on view. If, as I suggested earlier, one of the pentangle's connotations is its part in the construction of masculinity, what are we to make of the way that symbol is overlaid by this gorgeous, female item of clothing? The girdle is re-worded as a "drurye". It is something exchanged in an erotic context, by a man and a woman in a bedchamber after that lady has sexually propositioned the man. In such a light, Gawain's covert acceptance of it doubly implicates him.

His action impinges on 'trouthe'. It also taints his sexual propriety and propels him, however unknowingly or unwillingly, into a potential love triangle involving himself, the Lady and her husband, his host Bertilak.

The girdle thus operates as a magic charm *and* as an object of desire in a heterosexual frame. Or does it? The girdle accrues additional potential meanings when the Green Knight reveals himself as Bertilak and explains how their encounter has been engineered by Gawain's aunt Morgan, alias the old crone who accompanies the Lady at Hautdesert. Gawain responds by flinging the girdle in Bertilak's face and launching into an antifeminist tirade about the trickery of women (2378–428). He claims, too, that the girdle has made him forsake his true nature: that is, the generosity and "lewté [loyalty]" belonging to all knights. Some scholars concur with this, yet another re-signification whereby feminine values – represented here by the girdle – usurp, to its detriment, a chivalric code. Readings like this, however, ignore the fact that it is Gawain who interprets and condemns the girdle as a sign of female treachery; elsewhere, the poem suggests Gawain is not a trustworthy, clear-sighted reader of signs.

As the story progresses, meanings continue to slide. Bertilak picks up the girdle and re-presents it to Gawain who accepts it for a second time. Bertilak offers it as a souvenir of their battle, something to wear openly in the company of other aristocratic males (2395–99). In this sense, then, the girdle's signification slides from feminine to masculine. It now becomes a sign of chivalry after all, and, so, re-establishes the supremacy of masculine order – even though the poem continues to refer to it as a 'luf-lace'. Does 'lace' connote 'snare', as in the snare of love into which Gawain almost fell thanks to female duplicity? An interpretation like this insists upon the girdle as a heterosexual symbol of exchange. Yet the text plainly states that the same love token is not actually the Lady's, but belongs to Bertilak (2358), and more indirectly, to Morgan.

Before I consider the impact of this, I wish to turn to the poem's ending. Gawain accepts Bertilak's present of the girdle and, once more, re-signs it. He says he will wear it as a sign of his fault, in implicit contrast then to the 'trawthe' of the pentangle with which he started and which the girdle has seemingly over-written. To wear it like this will, he says, counteract pride and humble his heart.

Gawain insists the girdle is not itself a sign of pride, so he does not wear it out of vanity, for its beauty or its lavish workmanship (2429–38). Of course, in articulating what it is not, he also calls those possibilities into being. Gawain rides home to Camelot. He displays the girdle to all, a public sign, a "bend" or "baldric" worn over his right shoulder and tied under his left arm (2486–87). It is worn as a heraldic device, a diagonal band or 'bent' laid over a coat of arms. This perpetuates Bertilak's depiction of the girdle as a masculine, chivalric sign and, also, seemingly allies it with the pentangle, at this point absent from the narrative. So, too, the girdle functions as part of a chivalric ideal that Gawain fears he has undermined.

Once more, Gawain reworks the symbol to make it a "token of untrawthe" (2509), a sign of personal shame or dishonour that now circulates freely and openly in the public, homosocial world of Camelot (one predicated on fraternal bonds). This is a perfectly acceptable reading except for the fact that the heraldic mark the girdle finally 'becomes' matches no record of heraldic devices. Its public signification, then, is perhaps better read as one of absence, an attribute of the feminine. Equally, no one else in the court reads the sign in the way that Gawain intends it. They misperceive or ignore it as a symbol of shame. Instead, they laugh and re-write it yet again. Everyone wears a baldric in honour of Gawain's defeat of the Green Knight whose intrusion so rattled the Arthurian world.

Like the pentangle, the girdle is another symbol of unity and just as untrustworthy. While it literally laces Gawain's body, symbolically it keeps that body and his masculine identity together. At the same time, it sets up a series of affiliations that call that identity into question. To whom does the girdle belong – the Lady, Bertilak, Gawain, or Morgan? Why does it function in so many different ways and which – if any – fix it as a sign? Like other symbols and signs, the girdle's function is interdependent with so many other aspects of this text and its meaning is always contingent, always in the process of negotiation. This is not a fixed sign or one invested with clear or singular meaning. Like the pentangle and the Green Knight's greenness it seems integral to constructions of identity but the question is exactly whose subjectivity is at stake? Is it Gawain's? Is it that of social order where the behaviours and impulses of individuals both constitute *and* challenge communal identity? What, too, are we to make of Gawain's withdrawal from the court and, by implication, its values? Are we to re-read all signs and symbols in the light of that action, and/or in the context of the marvellous wreckage of history to which the poem finally returns us?

Other symbols

Orfeo's harp in *Sir Orfeo* is another central yet multivalent symbol whose significance alters in line with the variety of readings the tale prompts: Christian allegory, family drama, Breton lay focused upon the construction of art and culture, or perhaps a poem about death and the failures of dynasty. In classical and medieval times the harp's strings were said to replicate the divine music of the spheres. In this sense, then, the harp symbolizes harmony, becomes the sign of a stable, integrated cosmos. Orfeo is both a king and a minstrel, a skilled harpist whose instrument stays with him at all times. The harp first makes its appearance in the story after Orfeo's wife, Herodis, is abducted and he relinquishes the care of his kingdom to his loyal steward. Orfeo disappears into the wilderness, playing the harp only when the sun is up. When darkness falls, he hides it in a tree and all those creatures that came to listen to his music slink away (*Sir Orfeo*, 255–56). Orfeo neglects his duties both as a king and a musician. Instead of entertaining, he plays only sadly and intermittently, in mourning for his apparently dead wife. Having turned his back on the civilized world, he exists in abject, part penitential, exile. Here reality is fractured and the harp's power as a sign of order diminishes. That same heavenly music the harp produces was also associated with spirituality, according to medieval thinking. It is a sacred instrument, and thus signals that Orfeo's self-imposed retreat is a time of healing. In Christian readings, too, the harp indicates penitence, and so fits with the details of Orfeo in his pilgrim's cloak, barefoot, existing on a frugal diet of berries and fruit, his hair and beard grown long, everything reminiscent of the privations experienced by the saintly desert fathers of Christian theology (210–44, 255–56).

Orfeo's harp might also be seen as an entry/exit marker, a bridge between worlds, as well as a simple recognition token. Orfeo uses it to gain access to the faery 'hell' where Herodis is held. Posing as a minstrel, he is allowed inside. There his playing so delights the hall that the faery king grants him his heart's desire. Orfeo reclaims Herodis and returns to the real world he left behind ten years ago (385–455). He takes the harp into the city and plays for his former steward, now the regent of Orfeo's kingdom. The harp reminds the steward of his love for Orfeo (491–94). When the recital has finished, the steward asks how he came by the harp. Orfeo replies that he took it from a dead man, torn to pieces by wild animals in a far-off place. The steward's distress – he thinks the corpse is Orfeo – prompts the king to discard his disguise. Social order is reasserted when Orfeo takes up his kingship once more (496–525); the harp is no longer needed in the narrative and all mention of it now ceases.

The harp is, then, integral to a minstrelsy that simultaneously marks civilization or culture *and* tips us into a strange other-world where anything is possible. The entertainment enjoyed in the royal court is replicated in the faery kingdom. There, Orfeo glimpses the king and his retinue enjoying music and dancing (257–89). In the faery hall, Orfeo's harp music breaks the spell of suspended animation so that Herodis can be restored to life (435–42). Here the harp is a restorative suggesting life and regeneration, even as it remains central to the patterns of death-in-life and mourning in the tale. So, too, it signals entry in and out of the troubled, displaced state represented by faery, something that works in tandem with the more harmonious, ordering qualities of the harp.

Items of clothing often accrue symbolic meaning in medieval romance. Freine's cloak in *Lay le Freine* evokes a complex chain of associations in a story that inverts the 'fair unknown' motif common to many family-drama tales. The cloak functions as a multiple recognition token that enables Freine to claim the various identities – daughter, sister, lover, wife – that are key to her legitimacy. The notion of absence is crucial in this story, both its literal silences and the subtle ways in which women are written out of patriarchal scripts. Freine is an outsider. She is abandoned in the bole of an ash tree, wrapped in a beautiful "baudekine" or cloth. The cloak (and the ring found with her) is the only clue to her noble origins. When Freine comes of age, her surrogate mother, the abbess who raises her, gives her the cloak and the ring and tells how she was found. She advises Freine to keep them with her at all times. The objects have some material value but more importantly they are Freine's passport into another, better life. When Freine elopes with Guroun, she takes them with her. Much later, as she prepares a bridal bower for Guroun's forthcoming marriage to another, she decorates the bed with her own cloak. Her mother sees it, realizes who she is and the family are reunited.

Yet this is not simply a recognition symbol. The story of the cloak is not fully known until the end. There it does more than just flag Freine's identity. It intersects a host of ideas that resonate well beyond the tale's happy-ever-after and demand a retrospective of its unfolding. As befits the feminine slant of the tale, the cloak is made to represent absence in several ways. The cloak is presented to Freine's mother as a gift from her father. It is highly exotic, a fact that would particularly resonate for a medieval, Christian audience and add to Freine's status as an outsider beyond the safety of a patriarchal world. The cloth is from Constantinople (*Lay le Freine*, 137–44), a place associated with heathendom or Islam in contrast to the dominating force of the Catholic church, and a geographical entity at the edges of the civilized 'Christian' world. These connotations are exacerbated by the circumstances of Freine's abandonment. She is nameless, of the outside both literally (she is left in a tree) and metaphorically: the porter who discovers her at first sees only the cloak which he assumes has been dropped by thieves (190–99). To all intents and purposes, Freine is illegitimate and, hence, beyond the bounds of social order; this is why Guroun's fellow knights urge him to marry someone of rank (311–18). Secretly, however, Freine *is* nobly-born, as the cloak her mother left with her signifies, while Constantinople was also the centre of the eastern Orthodox branch of Christianity until it broke away to form its own church. The cloak's history thus renders it both same-as *and* other-to social order at one and the same time.

The cloak's conflicted status reaches its height in the bridal scene that marks the story's resolution. When Freine lays the cloak on the wedding bed, we are told this is to please Guroun (368). This explanation satisfies the demands of a masculine-dominated world, which privileges men but ignores the emotional resonance of the act. Freine prepares this bed for someone else who will take her place as wife. She thinks that the bed is too shabby for a honeymoon suite (360–62), though it has, metaphorically at least, been her own for she and Guroun have been living as man and wife. In some ways, the detail reminds us of the shabby treatment of Freine, good enough to be a mistress but not enough to wed. In placing the cloak on the bed, Freine re-evaluates her worth, as well as cueing her forthcoming legitimation. Once her mother realizes who she is, Freine can claim her family name and, with it, proper social honour. She is, at last, the bride whose bed demands lavish decoration and can leave behind her 'names' as lover, foundling, stranger, other. However, the cloak's significance continues to exceed its sign as order. It is a crucial symbol of movement, literally so in some cases. Written into its cloth is a sense of exile or estrangement. It travels from Constantinople to Brittany as part of a heritage of exchange. It accompanies Freine when she is taken from her home and abandoned outside the convent. From there, it is taken inside when Freine is claimed by the abbess, and then out again when she elopes. In the end, Freine passes it to Guroun's bride. On the surface, its journey is simple: home to exile to home, a trajectory that ends in reunion and upholds the principles of order. At the same time, its literal and its metaphorical shifts evoke a heterosexual paradigm as a legitimating force in society. Freine's father offers the cloth as a love token to his wife. His wife discards it, along with her baby, when she fears it calls to mind adultery. One of the effects of patriarchal order is that women are separated, often literally, and effaced. 'Daughter' has little value as a sign until she trades it for 'wife' and 'mother'. As an abandoned daughter, Freine is doubly erased. The cloak brings heterosexuality back into line when it reunites the family and secures marriage for Freine. What, then, are we to make of the discontinuities behind this apparent resolution?

The commodification and separation of women in patriarchy is usually effected via an exogamous exchange whereby men marry their daughters out of the family and into another family group. When Freine places the cloak on the bed, she, in fact, prepares it for her own sister, Codre. In effect, Freine, not her father, offers Codre to Guroun, and passes on her own role as quasi-wife to her twin. At the same time, she overwrites Codre's claim with her own to claim the *same* position. This double bind is evoked, too, in the literal twinning of the sisters, one inside the world and the other nameless, left out of it. Of Codre, the story says nothing. Once again, the cloak signals the dual status of women, articulated as full subjects only by becoming a wife and perpetuating the family name, and otherwise relegated to silence. When Freine lays the garment on the bed, she signs something of what is disavowed or written out in order for language and culture, a masculine world, to hold.

Emaré's robe is an especially nuanced and arresting romance symbol (see *Emaré*, 82–180). Like le Freine's cloak, it combines disruption, order, and recognition. Equally, its signification constantly slides even as it remains the one constant in a story where Emaré is always on the move, refusing and exchanging symbols through the robe that she keeps close to her at all times. When the king of Wales, Emaré's estranged husband, sees her in Rome, he only remembers who she is when the dress jogs his memory (933). Each time she is washed ashore after her enforced exiles at sea, she is wearing the same garment. In one sense, it displays her as victimized. Yet in another, because choosing to wear it is a deliberate act, it becomes as much a sign of agency as the way she changes her name, something designed to deflect attention and confound her origins. The robe, thus, bears a dual valency, recognition token and cloak of invisibility both.

The first thing anyone notices about Emaré is her clothing. Everyone sees the robe – and the woman in it – as something different, so that meanings clash and meld. Her father wants her to wear the dress as a wedding gown, thus revealing not only his own incestuous desires but the way in which, dressed in that robe, she seems to provoke high emotion in others. The merchant who rescues her from her second ocean voyage remarks how the glittering robe makes him believe she is not of this earth (697–701). Similarly, Sir Kador finds "a glysteryng thing" washed up on the Welsh shore in a dress so dazzling that its wearer seems not to be human (350), something echoed by her mother-in-law who thinks she is a fiend (445–47). In these instances, Emaré's robe doubles as a *misrecognition* symbol; none of the other characters are sure who or what she is and neither is the story's audience. This misrecognition is set in motion when her father, Artyus, tries to marry her. He has the gown fabricated for their nuptials, and literally pins on her a series of identities – alluring daughter, wronged daughter and, later, lost child. In contrast, when Emaré wears the same dress for her wedding with the king of Wales, *she* puts it on herself. This crucial difference allows her to overlay its earlier, disruptive potential, for at this point she is wearing it as an authentic, legitimate bridal dress and not being forced into an incestuous union.

There is no doubt that the robe bears all of these meanings at once. Its ambivalence stems from its origins. The gown that Artyus has made for his daughter comes from a bolt of cloth which took seven years to weave. The cloth is studded with gems from far and wide (115–20). The meaning of these stones is completely contradictory, ranging from chastity to lust (89–95). It is these gemstones which make her into a 'glistening' or 'glittering' creature. She literally dazzles in it and so metaphorically blinds everyone who sees her. By wearing it, she disorders knowledge and reason, two elements integral to masculine, symbolic order. It is also important to note that the robe can never, finally, constitute Emaré's identity. Rather, it is something she chooses to wear at certain moments of crisis to confound others. It is the dress that dazzles, not Emaré herself.

This same cloth also depicts the stories of a host of literary lovers, from Tristram and Isolde through to Floris and Blaunchflour. It testifies, too, to the love the Emir's daughter has for her chosen man. Their real-life love story is illustrated on the cloth which the girl later gives to her beloved (157–62). When the king of Wales first sees her in the robe, he instantly falls in love (400–03), thus reinforcing its potency as a love charm. Emaré's father, however, misappropriates that sign to shift it into another realm of signification altogether when he decides that he is in love with her. It is not until the reconciliation scene at the end of the poem, when husband and wife are reunited and the tragedy woven into its history deflected, that this token of love is restored to its proper place as a sign of marital affection.

The robe's potential to evoke illicit desire further complicates the scenario I have just described. Though it ends as an ordering sign, it begins as something entirely different. When he is given the cloth, Artyus declares it is "a fairy,// Or ellys a vanyté!" (104–05). His suggestion that the robe is an enchantment, some kind of erotic lure, is echoed throughout the tale. The Emir's daughter weaves love and desire into the cloth from the start. By presenting it to her lover in a moment of female agency, she makes the cloth doubly potentially transgressive. This girl is also a heathen and the cloth an exotic, eastern piece, all attributes that place it outside the bounds of an ordered, Christian world – just as, later on, Emaré will be exiled from that world, in part, on account of the robe. This, then, is a feminine and, hence, disruptive symbol, one that reverses natural order when it is passed from a woman to a man, and so conjures disturbing images of desire. Perhaps it is not surprising that her father is confused by it (101–02) and suddenly imagines his daughter as a sexual temptress (188).

When Emaré refuses his incestuous advances, her father casts her out, giving her up to the sea in a distorted version of traditional exogamy, before immediately regretting his actions and beginning a long search for the daughter – not the bride-to-be – he has lost. Interestingly, Emaré keeps the gown, thereby inciting further disruption on her travels. The robe becomes a literal sign of all that is illicit or potentially disordering, *and*, at the same time, symbolic of Emaré's *refusal* of these possibilities, a fixed sign of her virtue. Others continue to read her as supernatural in that dress. We are told that "she seemed non erthly thing" (396), but the emphasis is on 'seemed'. Though everyone who meets her is initially puzzled by her, they quickly come to love her. Right at the end, about to be reunited with the father who once forced her into the robe, for the first time in the story Emaré no longer wears it. Instead, she stands before him as 'Egaré' who once was Emaré, no longer his daughter with all the potential trouble that state might imply, but a wife and a mother (1003–08). The robe shifts its meaning, finally, from transgression to mediation and order.

The robe has, in many respects, been a fixed sign all along, a liminal disguise through which multiple meanings might be sifted, though perhaps never fully reconciled. We know that it is no faery thing, yet cannot forget its glittering, illusory allure. We recognize its part in the story's move from incest to proper, marital and family relations, even as the dysfunction it seems to incite permeates the tale. The robe bears the traces of a violent patrilinear history, its cloth an object of exchange won in battle by Sir Tergaunt's father, passed on to Sir Tergaunt and then presented by him to Emaré's father (169–80), before being shaped into a wedding gown to appropriate his daughter. Yet it began as a gift of love from a woman to a man, and is reclaimed in her own way by Emaré. The symbol that outlasts all others is that of Emaré in her robe, seemingly enchanted, in a dream-like exile afloat on the sea, a fixed, yet ultimately unreadable, feminine sign haunting the edges of the known world and exerting its own mysterious and compelling force.

The motifs and symbols repeated across these tales are a generic feature of romance, those often strange, sometimes highly visual details we all recall. Though they set up certain generic expectations or echoes that persist beyond individual stories, their significance is frequently multivalent and their meaning often ambivalent. Equally, meaning is often cumulative, part of the effects of other versions of a tale and integral to a thematic web of ideas and repeated allusions. We cannot read Freine's cloak, for example, without considering issues of identity, or understand Gawain's pentangle separately from other symbols or patterns of gender. Symbolic meaning is, then, far more than the simple matter of equating one sign with a conventional, often singular, representation. Alongside those general or popular meanings are other questions to be asked. Who has the symbol? How is it used or developed? What other connotations might it possess? From what position does the symbol speak?

CHAPTER 4

SCRIPTING IDENTITIES: PRIVATE AND PUBLIC WORLDS

STORIES OF ORIGINS

Family and kinship patterns are central to the foundation of western culture. Birth, marriage, reproduction and death structure our lives and play a crucial part in the way families interconnect, rear children and pass on property, moral values and cultural norms. A heterosexual kinship formation and its insistent replication apparently produce longevity and social stability. Most romances enact family dramas that script this ideology, while their formulaic happy-ends assert marriage and kinship as an ordering force. Along the way, the genre also holds this cultural foundation story up to the light, critiquing its smooth linearity – birth, maturation, marriage, children – via a series of disruptive moments or crises. Romance's recurrent themes – abandoned children, incest, rape, changelings, a search for name or origins – repeat, and so shore up, the ordering principles of heterosexuality, even as they gesture towards its problematic insecurity.

Kinship is, though, not merely a blood or social tie. In modern psychoanalysis it depends on the exchange of signs. In simple terms, 'daughter' belongs to 'father', for example. He will marry her out and away from the family in order to counteract her troubling, sexual presence and keep incest as a taboo. Once married, she is 'wife', the property of her husband and his family. Her value as sign increases if she becomes 'mother', especially the mother of sons. Sons inherit 'family', its name, lands and property, and pass it on to their own sons. In this way, patriarchy privileges and perpetuates a 'masculine' sign – the law, language, culture, religion, rationality, order – and writes out anything that is not part of this sign: same-sex or non-heterosexual desire, magic, anything feminine, silence, and so on.

Sir Degaré and *Sir Gowther* both dramatize the kind of family script I have just described, but do so in highly conflicted ways. Degaré's quest is to claim his kin so that he can enter the social world as a fully-fledged and recognized subject. To begin with, he is outside that sphere of influence, both literally and metaphorically. Degaré is only half-human for his father is a faery. He is also a foundling, born out of wedlock and abandoned without a name. The hermit who finds him christens him Degaré, meaning 'almost lost'. He educates him and, as he comes of age, prepares him for his quest to find "his kinrede" (*Sir Degaré*, 310) by handing him his patrimony: a letter from his mother, four pounds of gold and ten of silver, a pair of magic gloves and a broken sword left by his father (119–31). Degaré is, too, beyond the bounds of chivalric culture, something exemplified by his lack of horse and armour. Instead, he has a pilgrim's staff and a huge oak bat, rough-hewn from a tree in the same ancient woodland of his birth (325–34).

Degaré's inadvertent marriage to his own mother perpetuates his status as outsider, as well as having potentially devastating consequences for family bonds. The king's daughter, Degaré's mother, intuits this when she expresses concern over marrying a stranger, one whose birth and family background are unknown (585–92). The narrator interrupts to underscore its danger and warn that knowing the story of our origins is crucial in order to avoid incest (610–24). Yet even knowledge is sometimes not enough to deflect it. The king of Brittany so dotes on his daughter, Degaré's mother, that he kills all potential suitors and for 20 long years prevents her from marrying. The incestuous undertones of these actions are highlighted when Degaré's mother finds that she is pregnant after her 'faery' rape. Her comment that her father will be destroyed by this news "For al his joie is in me" (174) makes explicit his excessive, unnatural affection. Equally, she fears everyone will assume the baby is her father's and, so, they will lose their good name as a family (167–74).

The dysfunction of Degaré's family is the secret at the heart of this tale. The taboo desires of incest and rape deform kinship patterns and threaten the stability of society to keep its protagonists in psychological limbo where they are only half-known to themselves and each other, and where family bonds are disconnected. Thus Degaré's grandfather never articulates his feelings for his daughter.

Degaré's mother never speaks her desires either, so that Degaré's conception is half-rape, half- fantasy and the child's birth a shameful secret – not least because she knows nothing of the biological father's kin. Degaré's father is absent from the main part of the narrative, returning only at the end. His mother can tell him nothing of this 'man', save the partial story of his own origins, the broken sword by which he will be recognized. The magic gloves his mother leaves for him similarly show how the disordering effects of desire can only be repressed, never fully written out. Twice the narrative reminds us that these gloves are both a recognition token, fitting only his mother's hands, *and* a 'Cinderella' device to help find his true love (213–18, 311–16). Once Degaré's mother hears him explaining this to the king, his grandfather, she realizes who Degaré is and steps up to reveal their family connection. It is only then that the problem of their incestuous union is neatly side-stepped, pushed underground but not, finally, erased. The king of Brittany's behaviour towards Degaré's mother remains unexplained, a narrative hole that neither accounts for the odd nature of their long relationship, nor justifies its sudden disappearance.

The tale's doubled scenes go some way towards knitting up the conventional structures it seemingly avows. Degaré's final, coming-of-age battle is with a stranger who turns out to be his father. When Degaré's lance shatters against his opponent's shield to leave its point embedded there (1035–37), it replicates his father's own battle for maturity with a giant in whose head he lost the tip of the sword he later leaves for Degaré (124–31). This detail cues their recognition scene (1048–62) and the final piece of the family jigsaw. Degaré now has full chivalric status, a name, and a known family. His marriage to his mother is annulled on the grounds that they are too close kin (1093). His birth parents are reunited, their desire safely channelled into a proper sexual union. Yet what are we to make of his faery father's inexplicable entry into the real world, his supernatural origins entirely forgotten even though origins is precisely what this story is about? So, too, Degaré's marriage underwrites a narrative drive towards order even as it unsettles on account of its origins in faery. When Degaré leaves Brittany after the fiasco of his marriage to his mother, he encounters his future wife in an enchanted castle, deep in a faery forest. Her family drama parallels that of Degaré's mother. This girl also has an unwanted suitor threatening abduction who must be defeated if she and her realm are to survive. The tale's doubling motif underwrites the need to demarcate all that is proper – name, family, and its reproduction – in order to achieve full subjectivity. Yet in both instances, in Degaré's marriage and in that of his parents, that subjectivity is tainted by everything that faery, the social world's 'other', represents. I shall turn to discussion of liminality shortly; for now, it is perhaps enough to note that the story of origins in romance is a complex and uneasy one for all the apparent resolutions of its happy endings.

DYSFUNCTIONAL FAMILIES

Difficult questions about family, paternity and succession also frame the Middle English version of *Sir Gowther*. Gowther is kin to the devil. The story relates the consequences of that state and his eventual rehabilitation into society. At the start of the poem, Gowther's parents have been childless for many years. Gowther's mother prays to the Virgin Mary for a baby. Alone in an orchard, Gowther's mother meets a handsome, noble who looks exactly like her husband with whom she copulates. The man later shape-shifts into a hairy fiend and tells her that she has just conceived a child. In turn, she then tells her husband, the duke, that divine intervention has provided them with an heir (*Sir Gowther*, 73–99). Both the circumstances of Gowther's birth and his monstrous youthful behaviour reveal anxiety about paternity and legitimate inheritance.

Gowther passes as the duke's son. He is duly baptized, thus receiving an aristocratic family name. Later he is knighted. When the duke dies, Gowther inherits his title and lands exactly *as though* he was lawful, natural kin, and, so, perpetuates the duke's family line. There is, though, no doubting Gowther's paternity. Physically, he resembles his biological father while he is also said to be Merlin's half-brother (97–99). His behaviour is demonic, something beyond the bounds of chivalric culture. He participates in all the recognized rituals of that culture, its feasting, fighting, and hunting, yet does so in ways that exceed it. Gowther gorges on food, sucks dry several wet-nurses and tracks down and kills the vulnerable and dispossessed, or pillars of society like men of the church (106–204). It seems that natural kinship bonds will always prevail as Gowther rampages throughout the dukedom. When the old earl criticizes his lack of restraint and describes him as the spawn of the devil (205–12), he is articulating what everyone already secretly knows about Gowther's lack of proper social fit.

Gowther's wildness also calls attention to the covert structures of a society predicated on, and continually threatened by, those very oppositions that Gowther over-performs. His uncontrolled appetitive nature and violent desires remind us of the monster from whom he is descended and which sits at the heart of all foundational birth-stories. This is further exemplified by the suggestion that family name alone is not enough to confer nobility. No one nurtures good conduct in Gowther or checks his outrageous behaviour. While he is left free to do as he pleases, Gowther's mother flees the family home and shuts herself away in a castle (155–60); in so doing, she literally steps away from her proper, social roles – as mother, wife, even duchess. The duke publicly acknowledges Gowther as his son and rightful heir but fails to teach him how to live up to that name. Instead, he allows Gowther to lay waste to the family lands. The duke neglects, too, his wider paternal role, which is a duty of care to a dukedom that curses his son's – and, by implication his own – name. The duke worries and grieves but never acts. He eventually drops dead and, thus, leaves a gap into which Gowther steps (149–54).

Sir Gowther distorts those codes that pass as 'natural' and given. In so doing, it plays out what happens when individuals ignore their personal and social responsibilities, or take for granted behaviours and structures that only *appear* normative by reason of constant vigilance and repeated performance. Gowther can only redress past misdeeds and restore order when he enacts penance as a dog beneath its master's table. In the end, he sets aside the patrimony which is not rightfully his. He passes the dukedom on to the old man who cared enough for public order to question his paternity – and so inadvertently sparks Gowther's quest for a good name – and marries him to his widowed mother. Gowther weds the Emperor's daughter and takes up the rule of his father-in-law's empire in an effort to prove that commendable conduct is a necessary part of nobility. Order, it seems, is re-asserted. Or is it?

Gowther's birth father, absent throughout the main part of the narrative, remains outside conventional society, ignored but not, perhaps, entirely forgotten. His mother marries an old man with whom she is still unlikely to produce an heir and so perpetuates those problems for the dukedom which were there right at the start. Gowther is still part-demon by reason of his birth. Though he has effectively killed that aspect of himself, he remains drawn to all that is outside and unarticulated when he marries the miraculously recovered mute girl who cared for him while he was a dog. Gowther is, then, a strange reminder of the 'monster' lurking on the threshold of civilization, forever cast out, forever looking to come back in (see Part Three).

Western culture's greatest taboo sparks the popular romance *Emaré*. When Emaré's father falls in love with her, he immediately seeks to legitimate his disruptive, incestuous desire by making lengthy preparations for a marriage (*Emaré*, 229–40). Though marriage is usually a stabilizing sign in romance, here it deforms natural family bonds, as well as the emperor's obligation of paternal care to his kingdom. Emaré's refusal of him is an attempt to block this transgressive exchange of signs – daughter to wife – which would incite a twisted exogamy by failing to marry her out of the family. When she reminds her father that his proposed union will destroy their family name and his renown as a king (253–64), she spotlights the tremendous cost of breaking those seemingly solid laws. Her exile is a disaster for familial and personal relationships but seems the only way to safeguard an order that is finally knitted back together by the birth of her son Segramour, born with a double kings' birthmark to symbolize his future inheritance of the realms of Rome and Wales (504).

Chaucer's version of the same tale places special emphasis on the role of the family in cementing what psychoanalysis terms the symbolic order; that is the fully realized social world of language and culture. The tale is narrated by the Man of Law, a family lawyer. In the Prologue, he curses "horrible" stories of incest – of which his is one – and "unkynde [unnatural] abhomynacions", in a nervous refusal to acknowledge the taboo's foundational status (*Man of Law's Tale*, 77–88). The tale begins with Custance being sent away from her family in Rome to marry the Sultan of Syria. Custance's speech before she departs allows the narrator to stress women's proper place in conventional genealogy. Custance repeatedly refers to herself as her father's daughter or his wretched child (274–87, 1105–13). As such, she is his to exchange as he wishes. Yet she is also her father's sole heir, a value that increases once she gives birth to Maurice who is set to inherit the dynasties of Rome and Northumberland through her second marriage to Alla. In that sense, Maurice ties civilizations back together in exactly the same way as Segramour does in *Emaré*.

Maurice's role in patriarchy is more extensive than Segramour's, however. It is commonly assumed that patrilinear succession of this kind is perpetuated in its own image, that is to say almost literally, through a line of sons. Maurice's physical resemblance to Custance, rather than to his father, is significant for calling attention to the role of the mother whose value as sign increases in masculine-dominated society in accordance with her ability to provide sons and heirs. Custance uses Maurice to reconcile the family and draw together its complex kinship in a manner that clearly articulates her own crucial, linking role. She sends her son to Alla when he comes to Rome on a journey of penitence long after she has been exiled by his mother and when he believes her lost to him. As he looks upon this strange child, he is reminded of his estranged wife (1030–35). Later, he speaks to her of "Maurice my sone, so lyk *youre* face" (1063, emphasis mine). Custance's father also sees Maurice and wonders who he is, for the child puts him in mind of his long-lost daughter (1096). Even as Custance is cast out from Northumberland, she stands with Maurice in her arms and calls out to her husband in a public farewell that implicitly reminds everyone present that, as the mother of Northumberland's sole heir, she is a precious commodity they are throwing away (857, 861).

The Man of Law's insistence on the value of proper kinship is enhanced by the contrasting depiction of Custance's mother-in-law. Unlike her son's new bride, the Sultaness of Syria is old, her child-bearing days gone and her value as sign thus diminished (414, 432). The Sultaness also effectively ends the family line when she murders her own son, thus proving to the narrator that she wishes to usurp 'natural' order and rule in his stead (435). The Man of Law similarly outlaws Donegild as a 'mannish', hence unnatural, woman (782) and applauds Alla's action in killing her once he realizes she was responsible for the loss of his wife and son. Here, matricide restores order after Donegild's act of 'treachery' against the family line (890–96). The narrator's condemnation of Donegild and the Sultaness cannot disguise, however, the ambivalence and uncertainty of a kinship model he seeks to present as exemplary and secure. When Donegild forges the letters that, supposedly, legitimate Custance's exile, her terminology alerts the audience to Custance's dangerous potential as an unfixed sign. Who or what is she? Where is she from? What is her family background? Custance, like Emaré, refuses to tell her name, arrives from nowhere out of the sea and up-ends all the conventions of dynastic marriage. Donegild claims Custance is a "creature" (700). Later she calls her an "elf" (744), one arrived by chance or sorcery, and birth-mother of a fiend so horrible that everyone flees the castle (750–56). The Sultaness of Syria similarly fears that her new daughter-in-law will fracture the rules of rightful inheritance, despite the protracted legal proceedings of a union that brings together their two nations. In particular, that marriage demands that all of Muslim Syria must convert to Christianity, thus condemning everyone to hell in the eyes of the Sultaness (323–40).

In simple terms, Custance is not of their kind and her arrival disrupts taken-for-granted bonds about family, society, and, as I shall later discuss, religion and nationhood. The Man of Law overwrites these to assert a western, Christian paradigm of order. Yet his vehemence signals the instability of that order. In this context, instead of marriage regulating desire and, thus, safeguarding symbolic order, it, in fact, provokes disorder and undermines its own status as a fixed sign. One of the ways in which we see this in action is by examining the curious pattern of arousal clustered around the figure of Custance (and replicated in the symbol of Emaré's robe). She is presented as a near-holy, exemplary cipher, but that reading is counter-balanced by the feverish desire she seems to incite in others. The mere thought of a Custance revealed through the merchants' hearsay excites the Sultan of Syria so much that their wedding is said to be part of "hir bisy cure" (188). In Northumberland, Alla quickly falls in love (610–61), a jealous suitor tries to frame her for Hermengyld's murder (587–602), and, later, she has to fend off a potential rapist (913–23). Of course, the full significance of these events intersects other potential instabilities and readings. What is clear at this moment, however, is how in this case a tightly narrated account of a story is subject to the interventions and over-arching agenda of its clearly denoted teller (something relatively rare in romance), as well as to other, more extraneous influences.

WHAT'S IN A NAME?

Names and name-calling are crucial aspects of identity. To name or be named is how we are defined, how we step into culture as speaking, gendered subjects with a part to play – or not – in a conventional heterosexual dynamics. Naming is, too, integral to romance, which is driven by stories of how to get a name. A name and the personal and social identity it confers gains force by repetition. Thrown up onto the shores of Wales, and again back in Rome, Emaré refuses to tell her name. In one swift manoeuvre, she deletes her origins and establishes herself as an outsider, something beyond language – just as her shimmering robe confers a new identity as unearthly. So, too, Emaré re-names herself as Egaré. In the *Man of Law's Tale*, Custance also withholds her name even when her own kin, her uncle the senator, rescues her from exile (*Man of Law's Tale*, 970–73, 981–82). The meaning of these significant episodes is complex. On the one hand, they demonstrate a clear grasp of the mechanics of patriarchal and family law. Not-naming slips the Emaré-Custance figure into that state of absence occupied by women in masculine-dominated worlds. Here, they become completely other: without name, kin or place of birth, even possibly other-worldly fiends if their mothers-in-law are to be believed. When Custance claims to have lost her memory at sea (*Man of Law's Tale*, 526–27), she steps out of language completely. It is also possible that the gesture is a pragmatic one, a silence that ensures an amorous father, vengeful mother-in-law or callous husband cannot find her. At the same time, these silences encode the very traumas that produced them in the first place. This denial might also be viewed as a subversive action in that it demonstrates female agency. The central character chooses her moment – always during a literal arrival, a crisis point in the narrative – to evade masculine control and slip the bounds of social convention. From such a position, Custance and Emaré can rearticulate patriarchal laws. By withholding their family names, they refuse to acknowledge themselves as masculine property, whether as daughter or as wife. Instead, these women trade *themselves* to marry men of their own volition without enhancing their value by providing information about their family status. Ironically, in this way they compel and rework recognition. By changing their name, or refusing to give it at all, they delete one set of identification and set up another. The new then works in tandem with the old, unsayable connotation. We are prompted to fill in the gaps, to consider what is left out and why, including that emotional violence incurred when the protagonists lose themselves, those missing moments in the story such as when Custance sees Alla again, and in the depths of her heart recalls the pain caused by his behaviour in ostensibly casting her aside (1055–57).

Thus Custance and Emaré bear dual identities. They accept that they are recognized, named as daughters and wives, but also confer upon themselves identities as strangers. Emaré sends her son, Segramour, to the husband searching for her in Rome, commanding him to tell the king that her name is Emaré, changed to Egaré in Wales (*Emaré*, 956). In the reconciliation scene with her father, she greets him as Emaré who was his daughter, now named Egaré (1006–08). In this way, she ensures that she belongs to both *and* neither of these men. In the *Man of Law's Tale*, Custance names herself in a doubled family scene that frames the poem. As she prepares to marry the Sultan of Syria, a man chosen by her father, she articulates a pattern of kinship in which she has little worth. The cumulative force of her repeated 'father' and 'daughter' reminds us of the duty of care he owes her, even as he sends her off to a stranger (*Man of Law's Tale*, 274–87). She repeats the same terminology in the final reunion scene to bring the poem full circle. There she reiterates "fader" three times in the space of as many lines, together with "youre yonge child" or 'daughter' (1103–13). At the same time, she subtly shifts the tenor of the scene by simultaneously claiming Alla as her husband, thus showing that she both *is and is not* the Custance her father might recall.

SPEECH AND SILENCE: CULTURE AND LANGUAGE

Medieval grammarians and theologians theorized about speech and silence to invoke a binary of sound. What was described as scriptable sound is exemplified in both the printed word and intelligible speech. This is sound that is of the mind, rational and thoughtful, abstract ideas which are fully articulated and translated into direct speech, or else written as legible, recorded event. Scriptible sound (a technical term) is that which is either literally or metaphorically inscribed in what, according to medieval culture, was the correct way: corresponding to patriarchal Word and archived on a 'proper', whole body, thus giving us the body politic (state), law, and truth. This is also masculine sound, a privileged, safely bounded representation and understanding of the world. In contrast, non-scriptible sound is gendered feminine. Thus it is material or bodily noise, a corporeal language that emanates from deep within. It is associated with the senses – hence might be evoked by scent or touch – and with non-sense – laughter, tears, babble, physical gestures like swooning or bodily sounds such as flatulence or even silence, everything that was thought to leak from an open, female body composed of holes and entry/exit points. Non-scriptible sound is pure 'voice', acoustic noise or 'struck air'. Unlike scriptible sound, it cannot be fully represented in letters or print. Medieval thinkers likened such noise to that of a beast wandering unchecked, appetitive and monstrous. By also modelling it on the female body, they imputed to non-scriptible 'language' everything that same body represented for medieval theology: gluttony, excess, irrationality, unbridled female sexuality and corruption. Such sound might include hearsay, gossip or other oral markers increasingly denigrated with the advent of print culture and opposed to the singular truth of the Word of God. Non-scriptible sound is potentially always sinful, a manifest spiritual failing to transcend corporeality or comprehend God's Word (Sturges, 2000: 80–89). In literary terms, then, scriptible sound carries the authority of print, manuscript, carefully inscribed letters or else masculine speech: that is lawful, logical, singular and clear in meaning. Non-scriptible sound is unrepresentable. Instead, it exists in literary texts as a series of seemingly irrational, indirect or ambivalent pulsions, perhaps silences or that which is disavowed yet still lurks at the edges of a story.

This medieval binary also partially maps onto contemporary psychoanalytical theories. Julia Kristeva, for instance, delineates a paternal or masculine symbolic as a space in which we construct identities. So, too, we think about and structure our worlds by naming and appropriating objects to fix them and bring them into language. This symbolic order is homogeneous and authoritative, the known public world of language, culture and society. In order to circumscribe this world, however, we must first repress and deny what Kristeva calls the feminine semiotic, what other theorists term pre-Oedipal. This is the space of mother–child unity, full of bliss (*jouissance*) and desire, a heterogeneous and sensual place. Like the realm of the non-scriptible, it is modelled on the female body and gives us a similar range of sounds: tears, laughter, babble, rhythm, poetic language as well as obscenities and bodily noises. This kind of sound is expelled (abjected) in order that we can enter the symbolic, its spell broken in favour of singular meaning and paternal, authoritative laws. Kristeva points out that even though we repress the semiotic, we continue to desire it. This desire might express itself as a series of spontaneous, uncontrolled eruptions or pulses in language, or texts, thus demonstrating the fragility of scriptible, symbolic order (see Kristeva, 1980: 133–36).

I have spent some time explaining these ideas in order to use them as a lens through which to think about a range of medieval romances. We see, for example, these oppositions at work in *Emaré* and the *Man of Law's Tale*. Both of these stories stress the legal and papal dispensations necessary to effect marriage and show masculine, scriptible word in action. The Man of Law writes Custance through biblical miracles, exemplary silence and examples of holy virtue. Yet, all the time, we read this against the non-scriptible evasions I have been tracing: the symbolic meanings of Emaré's gown, hidden 'Accursed Queens' and incest analogues, everything the narrators cannot, or will not, recount about the strange compelling silence of exile. The tales of *Sir Orfeo*, *Lay le Freine*, and *Sir Gowther* are similarly conflicted by ideas about scriptible speech and its resonant opposite.

Sir Orfeo emphasizes silence, physical gesture and music to ensure that the poem continually elides authoritative meaning. When Herodis first dreams of the fairy world and its promise to claim her, she is unable to explain anything about what she has envisioned. Of course, faery has a semiotic force all of its own with its silences, gaps and wonders beyond the perception of a logical, human mind. Accordingly, when she wakes, it seems that Herodis has gone mad. She emits horrible cries which continue even as she is restrained and placed in her bedchamber. She can only speak her distress in non-scriptible terms that enhance the power of her visions: she tears at her clothes, scratches her face and body and rubs wildly at her hands and feet (*Sir Orfeo*, 53–58). So, too, she is unable to speak only in private to Orfeo, alone in their room. The masculine symbolic world, with its public demonstration of law in the shape of a thousand armed knights, has no power to protect her, and Herodis disappears into a literal silence (167–70).

When she next sees Orfeo, they are both in a dream state and unable to communicate with words. Herodis weeps to witness the man her husband has become (295–306). On the subsequent occasion of their meeting, she is freeze-framed in the exact pose of her first sleep under the enchanted imp-tree (363–84), when she is, in all senses, now lost to Orfeo. After Herodis's abduction, Orfeo likewise retreats into a semiotic space. He cannot stop weeping. This is the response too of his subjects when Orfeo renounces his kingdom

(177–212), a detail that highlights the extent to which events have disordered the social world. For ten years, Orfeo neither sees nor speaks to anyone. That profound silence is only punctuated when he plays his harp to the birds and the beasts of the forest; when the music ceases, even they shun him (255–56). In this long silence, Orfeo and Herodis seem dead to each other, and to the wider world. It allows us to contemplate the nature of a symbolic order distorted in the parallel dimension of faery where its masculine, scriptible authority is fractured. The faery universe is a defamiliarized version of real life (see 257–89). The paralysis of its fallen world is a spell broken not by masculine law in the shape of an army, but by the feminine, non-scriptible sound of Orfeo's harp. His music restores everyone to life and enables him to reclaim Herodis, re-enter language and culture and return home (385–455).

This music is not, as we might expect, simply an inferior value set against its privileged opposite, the scriptible word. Orfeo's playing is a recognized and integral part of the same symbolic order to which he returns, and not its expelled other half. A disguised Orfeo plays to his steward who is thinking all the time of his former king (491–94). Orfeo is so skilful that everyone stops to listen. When the steward asks where he found the instrument he is playing, Orfeo says he took it from one torn to pieces in the wilderness. The steward is so distressed that he swoons. This physical, non-verbal response is the moment that Orfeo reveals the true story (495–525); language, thus, recuperates social order and Orfeo takes up his rightful place as king again.

Equally, though, non-scriptible – represented by the harp – is also integrated into that world as a necessary sign. The harp is 'struck air' at exactly the same time as it is valorized as scriptible authority. There, it is reminiscent of biblical kings and prophets. In classical and medieval writings, too, its strings represented the divine music of the spheres and, thus, a stable integrated cosmos. Certainly, Orfeo can only defeat the faery king and restore civilization through his harp music. How secure is the ending of *Sir Orfeo*, though? The final words may yet be non-scriptible. Herodis disappears from the narrative. The harp's symbolism is multiple and ambivalent. The central myth of Orpheus that this romance riffs on – and to which I shall return – indirectly impacts on the romance version offered here. Ultimately, perhaps, silence speaks more powerfully than words.

The entire plot of *Lay le Freine* hinges on silence. Ostensibly, the story foregrounds the role of the family and the way in which marriage regulates desire in order to secure patriarchal order. In so doing, it also reveals the emotional costs these structures incur. The tale is marked throughout by oral and non-scriptible features. When her neighbour gives birth to twins, Freine's mother maliciously repeats an old wives' tale. Here the arrival of twins signals that two different men have fathered these children, meaning that one of the babies must be from an adulterous relationship and, hence, illegitimate. When she later has twins herself, Freine's mother fears slander of the kind she has invoked earlier and, so, plots to kill one of them. Instead, the midwife takes Freine and abandons her on the steps of a convent. Within the first 50 lines, then, the story touches on adultery, infanticide, illegitimacy and child abandonment, all through the mechanics of hearsay, gossip and private, female secrets – even as it immediately expels them to the realm of silence.

The power of such a narrative swerve is immense. Freine's secret birth story, already seated at the heart of the plot, is doubly silenced when the abbess takes her in and pretends that she is her niece. Though the abbess later reveals to Freine the circumstances in which she was found – and passes on the cloak which is the secret mark of her origins – silences accumulate to keep Freine outside the structures of symbolic order. Similarly, Guroun enters the convent under the guise of seeking instruction, only to seduce Freine and persuade her to elope. The pair then co-habit. That Freine lives as his wife is an open secret among his peers. Yet his fellow knights pressurize Guroun to marry someone of acknowledged rank and to discard Freine whose birth story is unknown (*Lay le Freine*, 311–18). Guroun's bride turns out to be Freine's twin sister, and, when their mother recognizes the cloak she left with her abandoned baby, the silence of the past is finally brought into scriptibility.

In this way, the non-scriptible secret of Freine's birth is kept in view throughout. The story continually moves it into the light, uncovering the missing pieces sequence by sequence until Freine can claim her name and re-assert scriptible law. When she and Guroun at last marry and she is brought back into the family fold, it seems that, finally, she is a fully articulated, speaking subject recognizable to herself and to all those around her. Once again, though, this too-neat ending over-writes any disquiet about the legitimation of desire impelling the plot.

What are we to make of the force of a non-scriptible, 'feminine' – whereby malicious speech can turn back on the person making it – and Freine's fearful mother is driven to separate herself and her girls? Guroun is allowed to seduce Freine, have her as his mistress, abandon and then reclaim her in a single act of reparation; we know nothing of Freine's reaction to this. So, too, there is resounding silence over Freine's emotion when she learns that her man will wed another, or that her mother gave her up at birth while her sister, Codre, is forever absent from the narrative. The cumulative effect of Freine's status as nameless foundling, lost twin and daughter, secret 'niece' and mistress-wife is to keep her cut off from a real world that then silently re-absorbs her back into a tale where non-scriptibility actively shapes meaning and seems far more resonant than its scriptible, plotted events. Above all, even though Freine is centred as the title of this poem, she only speaks directly a short time before the end. Only when her mother identifies her and gives her a name can she step into the symbolic world to gain legitimacy, kinship, marriage – and speech. Until then, she is absent from her own story, thus telling us something of the status of women and, more specifically, of daughters, in masculine-dominated society.

SECRETS AND LIES

Earlier, I suggested that how others speak us is as important as how we speak ourselves, for both are crucial to the ways in which we construct subjectivity. Most scriptible acts, spoken and written, attempt to put something in place. In this manner, they constitute a circuit of exchange that simultaneously constitutes *and* threatens our existence. As my discussion of *Lay le Freine* shows, one of the ways this might occur is when the use of silence, suppression and non-verbal, non-scriptible eruptions into language exert their own, parallel constituting force. Another way is through injurious or 'excitable' speech. This kind of speech may be articulated – and, thus, scriptible – or be hearsay and gossip; it name-calls – literally so in some cases – to compel a particular recognition or impose an identity. It may also miss its mark or even turn back its force against the one who speaks it. In both instances, such silencing or misrecognition leaves a residual identity that, like Emaré's change of name, hovers over what is openly scripted or acknowledged (see Judith Butler, 1997: 1–5, 29–35). I introduce this idea at this point in order to move on to discussion of the ways in which a speech–silence axis apparently splits some romances in two, even as it is the foundational pivot upon which they all turn.

On the surface *Sir Gowther* is another romance tale about how to claim your name. It traces how Gowther, born to the secret 'outside' of symbolic order, must learn the lessons of restraint, good conduct and properly regulated desire if he is to take his proper place in a masculine world. The catalyst for this re-entry into civilization and culture comes when Gowther overhears gossip about his demonic origins. The suggestion that he is not the duke's natural son blows apart the workings of a symbolic order in which men confer names and titles that can never finally fix or fully constitute identity. To begin with, the duke claims Gowther as his own kin; he knights him and names him as his legitimate successor in a process that apparently acknowledges Gowther as a fully fledged subject. Yet Gowther is both the target and instigator of excitable speech. The tale, thus, demonstrates that notions of identity and communal well-being are both far more friable than we might like to believe.

Once again, a non-scriptible realm underpins a story about naming. Gowther's kinship is predicated on secrecy and falsehood. His mother conceives him with a demon. She subsequently professes he is her husband's son, born of divine intervention and foretold to her by angelic prophecy. This lie uses the authority of scriptible law – its biblical roots augment its power – to embed a central untruth in the duke's lands. Seemingly, it is easier to accept and authenticate an unseen miracle with the power of scriptible speech than it is to sanction secret desire, adultery or bastardy. Because of this, though the duke knights his 'son', the identity he confers is precarious at best, and susceptible to non-scriptible forces. What is worse, Gowther's behaviour publicly fails to live up to the demands of chivalry, instead reverting to the 'natural', non-scriptible legacy of his faery father.

Gowther's actions are non-scriptible in the sense that they are material or bodily events that place him outside the jurisdiction of masculine, symbolic law. He rapes virgins and wives alike, as well as raping a convent full of nuns before locking them in and torching the building (*Sir Gowther*, 196–97, 181–92). As a result, the dukedom curses Gowther's name (161–65). The plain-speaking earl inadvertently stumbles on the truth when, on behalf of the community, he curses Gowther – and presumably the duke's entire family line – when he tells him that his son is the spawn of the devil (205–12).

Gowther reacts with anger, threatening injury to the earl (205–16). Likewise, he demands the name of his father from his mother at knife-point (220–24). The devastating consequences of society's failure fully to suppress the disruption of Gowther's non-scriptible birth are not only witnessed in Gowther's wild behaviour. His mother abdicates both her allegedly natural, maternal role and a wider social position as duchess when she locks herself away in a far-off castle (155–66). Literally, she is silenced. Nothing more is heard of her until a passing reference at the end when she is reclaimed for scriptible law and married to the old earl who first questioned Gowther's paternity. Gowther's 'father' the duke also retreats into non-scriptibility, internalizing his profound distress over the havoc his son wreaks and literally worrying himself to death (149–54). The duke also steps aside from his duty of paternalistic care, both to Gowther and to his dukedom, leaving it beyond the bounds of order and allowing Gowther to continue his destruction of it.

The secret of Gowther's birth thus has public consequences. In order for this to be redressed, Gowther must enact penance in both scriptible *and* non-scriptible worlds, for the two remain inextricably joined, before finally rewriting it for authoritative, masculine law. This textual manoeuvre occurs when Gowther becomes an elective mute serving his master as an abject dog and, also, as the secret champion of the Three-Day tournament. Gowther's state at this time parallels that of the emperor's daughter who is the only one to recognize his dual, public–private identity as both dog and knight. She is apparently dumb, a condition which will take a miracle to cure, according to her father (388–95). That miracle is love and it also enables Gowther to be 'cured' of his wild streak. When he is injured fighting in the tournament, the girl falls from a tower. She lies in a coma for three days then suddenly recovers. Her voice has returned and with it she can identify Gowther as their champion (661–66). Once the pair marry, Gowther's time in a personal wilderness is complete; he returns as a reformed character, 'domesticated' like the dog he once was. He is made heir to the empire and now speaks and behaves with the courtesy his position demands.

Yet, as with so many romances, this assertion of order is perhaps too easily achieved. The monstrous violence of Gowther's childhood and youth is far more vivid than the rehearsed, conventional contrition at the end of the poem. When Gowther marries his widowed mother to the old earl who originally challenged the duke, it is a marital arrangement that effaces the troubling excitement of her demonic rape. So, too, the parallel way in which both Gowther's mother and the emperor's daughter retreat into silence, and, by the end, vanish completely from the story, raises a host of questions about what might be articulated from the subjugated position of those outlawed from symbolic order, left without a proper identity or even a name.

SLANDER AND DEFAMATION I

If *Sir Gowther* leaves us wondering how those excluded voices might speak, *Sir Launfal* brings them centre stage. *Sir Launfal's* opening lines list Arthur's Round Table knights (*Sir Launfal*, 10–25) to draw up a scriptible, masculine universe that the poem then critiques. There is an immediate tension between public and private speech and behaviour when we learn that this same glorious Arthurian court conceals the open secret of the queen's promiscuity (44–48). Rumours of it are rife and threaten to rupture public order. Launfal's exile to Caerleon replicates this same structuring binary. The letter explaining his father's death and Arthur's lavish leave-taking apparently confirm and perpetuate scriptible, fraternal bonds. This public spectacle conceals, however, another impetus for Launfal's removal from public life, which is, of course, Guinevere's open repudiation of him during the gift ceremony that marks the occasion of her marriage to Arthur. Though this is enacted in full view of the court – and is, therefore, fully legible to it – no one will speak of Launfal's shaming. Instead, there seems an unwritten agreement to consolidate Launfal's status. Similarly, Hugh and John publicly praise Launfal when they return to Camelot (157–68), and conceal his poverty-stricken, dishonoured state exactly as he asked them to (142–44). So far, it seems that as long as gossip circulates privately and stays in a non-scriptible realm, then a masculine symbolic can hold. However, this reading is far from being the sum of this tale, for Launfal's successful re-entry into chivalric society is confirmed in scriptible speech *at exactly the same time* as it also turns upon the idea of silence.

In the invisible, unwritten world of faery, Tyramour pledges love, material aid and eternal life. In return, Launfal must never speak of her or bring her into scriptibility (315–65). Their promise replicates the troths and bonds through which chivalry is secured. When Launfal finally breaks his vow, its effect is to damage everyone concerned.

Launfal's failure to keep his promise imputes not only his own integrity but that of the entire Arthurian world. Significantly, Arthur recalls Launfal to Camelot on the basis of non-scriptible hearsay rather than assured knowledge or worth proved in open court (613–18). Arthur's action, together with Launfal's subsequent return, sparks a series of injurious exchanges that thoroughly disorder civilized society when the open secret about Guinevere can no longer be ignored.

The unravelling of social ties begins with Guinevere's private declaration of love to Launfal (649–54). When he refuses her, Guinevere imputes his masculinity. In return, Launfal tells her about Tryamour (685–99). The exchange escalates when Guinevere accuses Launfal of treason; she publicly declares that *he* propositioned *her*, Arthur's queen, as well as claiming that his beloved's ugliest maid could usurp order and rule in her place (715–20). Guinevere's slander is, of course, a lie but its effect is far reaching. Not only does it seek to destroy Launfal's reputation for honour but, perhaps more importantly, it threatens to rewrite legible order by making 'trouthe' (one's word) and truth collide. Everything that is non-scriptible is suddenly on the brink of becoming public. A lie might overwrite truth. An angry and petty private exchange is made public and, in so doing, is rewritten. Personal 'trouthe' slides. Arthur's pledged, marriage 'troth' to Guinevere conflicts with public duty and the renown of the Round Table. Launfal breaks his vow to Tryamour in order to save face, while Launfal's public trial is shaped by a common, yet always unspoken, knowledge of Guinevere's promiscuity (790–92).

Interestingly, the situation is resolved not by exiling Launfal as his fellow knights suggest (846) – and, so, sidestepping all of the above issues – but by allowing non-scriptible secrets fully into the real world. From nowhere, Tyramour and her retinue of exotic maidens burst into Launfal's trial scene (925–66). When Tryamour removes her mantle, she re-scripts her invisibility and allows everyone to see her (979–81). Arthur breaks faith with Guinevere to agree that Tryamour is lovelier (1003–05). Earlier, Guinevere boasts that she will put out her eyes if this should be the case (809–10). Her abusive speech turns back upon her when Tryamour breathes on Guinevere and blinds her (1006–08). The damage to accepted codes of behaviour is colossal. Masculine scriptibility is overturned by an assertion of feminine, non-sense, is completely let down by a public order and code of honour that cannot be sustained. Launfal disappears into the silence of faery (1035). His annual return is a jeering challenge to anyone who wants to keep their armour from rusting (1028). It reminds that court of its shaky, compromised foundations and us of the hollowness at the heart of all civilized society.

SLANDER AND DEFAMATION II

The closing books of Malory's *Morte Darthur* hasten towards king Arthur's death and the break-up of the Round Table fellowship. Civil disorder is unleashed when the malcontents Mordred and Agravayn decide to foreground the unacknowledged rumour of Guinevere's affair with Lancelot. Malory implies that Arthur was aware of the hearsay surrounding his queen and his best knight but chose not to act. He writes that the king was reluctant to hear "such a noyse" about the two, especially when he recalls his affection for a man who has done so much for him and Guinevere (*Morte Darthur*, 674).

Arthur's dilemma is mired in romance's subtle negotiation of the complexities of speech and silence. Though the constant circulation of "noyse" always threatens to undermine the stability of the Arthurian court with its complicated affiliations of kinship and honour, so long as everything remains unspoken then danger might be averted. Once injurious speech, in the shape of public slander, becomes the fellowship's watchword, everything can only unravel. The descent into, first, unrest and, then, civil strife or chaos is marked by an increasingly sharp distinction between scriptible and non-scriptible sound. Agravayn and Mordred foment discontent by speaking openly of Arthur's shame; they plan to reveal the alleged affair so that many can hear of it (673). Gawain acts as spokesperson for a majority when he refuses to countenance their actions. He reminds them of Lancelot's repute: his knightly prowess, the many times he has saved the lives of the king and his queen, and of Gawain, Mordred and Agravayn too, let alone the loyalty he commands amongst the Round Table fraternity. Gawain's insistence on detailing Lancelot's noble deeds and kindnesses privileges a different kind of hearsay over scandal-mongering and rumour, one of public reputation founded on and shored up by repeated, oral commentary. Gawain concludes by repudiating idle gossip: he "woll nat here of youre talis" (674). When, later on, Arthur asks them all "what noyse they made" (674), Agravayn defies Gawain's advice and tells of Lancelot's supposed treachery. Despite his private inclinations, Arthur publicly rejects any notion of treason. He demands proof, will only be satisfied if "he be takyn with the dede" (674). In this context, speech of any kind has little value. Without clear action, Lancelot will, says Arthur, stir up "the noyse" and deny everything (674).

Increasingly "noyse" connotes not simply slander or rumour but literal shouting, sound that deflects rational sense in favour of non-scriptible agitation and hot-headed words that, nevertheless, seek to bring private behaviour or dialogue fully into an open arena. So, Mordred, Agravayn and their followers gather outside the queen's private bedchamber where they cry out accusations of treason "with a lowde voice" so that the entire court can hear (676–77). At the same time, fair words and masculine courtesy make little impact on the injurious verbal exchanges between Lancelot, Arthur and Gawain. The king publicly curses Lancelot's attempts to resolve the conflict and restore both his and Guinevere's reputations. Arthur shouts "Fye upon thy fayre langayge!" (688), even as in private he weeps to think of Lancelot's esteem and the havoc wreaked by their war (691, 693, 694). Gawain also rejects chivalrous talk and, with it, everything that was formerly privileged as masculine, scriptible speech. When Lancelot insists that Arthur has been listening to 'tales' and 'lies', Gawain refuses further explanation with the command "Make thou no more langayge" (697). Instead, Gawain makes everyone shout in unison that Lancelot is a "false recrayed [cowardly] knight" (690).

The continued denigration of scriptible language parallels the complete breakdown of Arthurian order. More and more, non-verbal gestures signal the collapse of authority and a disorder both emotional or personal, and social. When Lancelot unwittingly kills Gawain's beloved younger brothers – and his own, most loyal follower in Gareth – Arthur unsuccessfully tries to draw a veil of silence over the event, knowing that it will provoke all-out war (685). The king weeps and "sowned [swooned]" (685), as does Gawain once he realizes what has occurred (686). In the middle of one battle, when Lancelot once again spares his life, the king looks upon his favourite knight and "the teerys braste oute of hys yen" (691). Arthur cries too when Lancelot agrees to return Guinevere to him (693), while throughout the realm there is much weeping on both sides (694).

This prolonged civil conflict "was noysed thorow all Crystyn real-mys"; the rumour even reaches the pope (692). The devastating force of hearsay and oral tidings gathers pace, moving out from personal to national or 'English' strife and across into Christian Europe. In an effort to restore order, the pope sends one of his bishops to Arthur with papal bulls charging him to take back his queen and make peace with Lancelot. For a brief moment, it seems that scriptible authority can repair the damage of non-scriptible upheaval. Arthur is willing to accede to the pope's request but Gawain's personal grudge against Lancelot over the death of Gareth takes precedence over public good and a king's jurisdiction. Accordingly, Arthur writes that he will be reconciled with Guinevere and allow Lancelot safe passage only for the duration of the journey to bring her home. This formal assurance is stamped with the king's seal and shown to Lancelot who accepts its conditions (692–93).

The respite proves short-lived. After delivering Guinevere, Lancelot flees to France with Arthur and Gawain in pursuit. Left behind as Arthur's regent, Mordred – Arthur's bastard son, born of accidental incest with Arthur's half-sister – takes advantage of their departure to stake his unwritten and unlawful claim on the crown. In addition, he declares his intent to marry Guinevere who, if Mordred is to be believed, has just been widowed. Mordred forges letters confirming Arthur's death at the hands of Lancelot and is crowned in his place. Guinevere's "Fayre speche" deceives Mordred into allowing her to travel to London, apparently in preparation for their nuptials (707). Once there, she takes refuge in the Tower of London. No one speaks out against Mordred's seizing of the crown and the subsequent disruption to the divine right of kings or legitimate succession. Similarly, only the Archbishop of Canterbury protests against his plan to wed Guinevere by reminding him of the law prohibiting the marriage of close kin: Mordred is Arthur's son and nephew, making Guinevere his aunt and his stepmother. Mordred's response is simply to curse the Archbishop 'with book, bell and candle' (708). Here, non-scriptible pulsions disorder every authority imaginable. Scriptible language is made pliable, subject to vested interests and not to moral truth or affirmed legislation. Hearsay increasingly proves more effective than a written or courteously spoken word which cannot be trusted. So, those in France hear rumours and "tydyngis" of Mordred's behaviour and effect a swift return to England (707). Mordred like-wise hears gossip about Arthur's homecoming and so serves writs upon Arthurian bishops and nobles to make them stand in his favour. Interestingly, rumours have so mingled that "the comyn voyce" of the land is that Arthur's reign has brought not glory but strife (708).

The constantly shifting balance of a speech–silence binary is further up-ended at the close of the *Morte Darthur*. The value of the written word is *seemingly* upheld when, on his deathbed, a contrite Gawain scripts a letter to Lancelot, telling of his love for him and urging him to return to England to save the king (710). Similarly, Arthur legislates for a month's treaty with Mordred. Yet, once more, that 'word' is false, this time a ruse to allow Lancelot to travel back from France. It is also an action prompted by non-scriptible dream-lore; the ghost of Gawain comes to Arthur in a dream and warns him not to meet with Mordred on the field the following day for he will be killed (711–12). Equally, when Arthur draws his sword to kill the adder that has just bitten him, that non-verbal gesture is read as an act of aggression and the truce disintegrates. In the subsequent battle, Arthur goes to kill Mordred who fatally wounds him in return (712–14). Guinevere retreats into silence, escaping to a nunnery where Lancelot dreams – correctly as it happens – that she dies. Arthur is taken in a barge by the women of Avalon, back to a mythical realm. The Arthurian story-cycle ends, but not quite.

Malory's narration of this part of his book compounds the collapse of scriptible authority and, with it, of the foundational structures of chivalry. To begin with, he elides the fact of Guinevere's adultery, which is the very thing that cues the end of Arthur's rule. One of Malory's sources is the French romance writer Chrétien de Troyes. In 'The Knight of the Cart', de Troyes is unequivocal about the nature of Lancelot's relationship with the queen. When Melegaunt holds her captive, Lancelot breaks the bars of her bed chamber window to spend the night with her. In so doing, he severely injures his hands, leaving blood-stains all over the bed sheets as tangible proof – at least according to Melegaunt – of their sin. Chrétien de Troyes also tells how Lancelot declares he wishes to hold Guinevere in his arms before he dies: "And how? Certainly, with both of us naked for my greater pleasure" (see Chrétien de Troyes, *Arthurian Romances*, trans. D.D.R. Owen, J.M. Dent, London, 1987 rep. 1993, 241). He writes too that the queen warmly welcomes Lancelot into her bed because she loves him; once there, "They truly came to experience such joy and wonderment . . . but of that I shall keep silent, since it should not be told in a story" (247).

Malory repeats this incident to note how Lancelot takes "hys plesaunce and hys lykynge" with Guinevere (*Morte DArthur*, 657) When Malory narrates how the rebel knights surprise Lancelot in Guinevere's chamber, he cites "the French book" to confirm that the pair are together, though whether in bed or "at other maner of disportis" Malory will not say. He continues to elide the issue of actual adultery by adding that love in those times was not as it is nowadays (676). This narrative explanation is ambiguous. Does he mean that their love is so noble that to reveal details of its consummation – or not – demeans it? Or that sexual standards were different in Arthurian times – and if so, to what end is he telling us this? Certainly, he implies that there is an element of doubt – not so earlier – about the precise nature of a relationship deemed so scandalous that it brings down the entire Arthurian realm. So, too, Malory deliberately confuses sources in his account of Arthur's death. According to him, Arthur's death is never committed to print as an actual fact: "Thus of Arthur I fynde no more written in bokis that bene autorysed" (717). The Archbishop of Canterbury is recorded as saying that a body believed to be Arthur's was brought for him to inter, a "tale" that is "written" as truth, though the bishop cannot verify the identity of the corpse. Malory further obfuscates by switching source books at this moment and, thus, undermining any notion of scriptibility as a secure, and positive cultural force. So, in England, others say that Arthur is not dead, that he will come again and win the Holy Cross; elsewhere, "Men say" – a repeated phrase – that Arthur's name is inscribed on a tomb, and, so, by implication, he must be dead (717). Some English books mention that Lancelot's followers and kin never leave England once *he* is dead. The French sources, or so Malory claims, say they went to the Holy Land, as Lancelot wished them to, where they fought 'miscreants' and 'Turks' (726).

It seems that, for Malory at least, the propriety, or otherwise, of Lancelot's relationship with Guinevere is less important than the loose talk it incites and the subsequent destruction of Arthurian order. Instead, he laments the passing of an era that he sees as a model for an English nation, cursing the "new-fangill" folk who shift allegiance so readily to side with Mordred (709). Why are Englishmen, he asks, unable to perceive the mischief at work in slander of this kind? What holds now, he states, is an old custom of discontent; the greatest fault of Englishmen is that nothing pleases them for long (708).

IN SPACE AND TIME

The medieval world conceived of space as simultaneously concrete and symbolic. Space comprised actual locations or geographical entities – forests, fields, gardens, castles and so on – *and* imaginary spaces as loci for fears, dreams, desires or simply stories. Medieval ideas about time were similarly paradoxical. Diurnal (daily) time was strictly marked by a liturgical calendar of feast days, bell times and calls to prayer or Mass and also by the seasons, especially in rural areas. Historical time co-existed with the real, actual time I have just described. Historical time was conceived in two ways. The first was real time past events or historical 'facts'. The other was legendary, the story time of myths or invented things. Sequences of actual kings or bishops might then be recounted alongside stories of pagan empires, the founding of Britain by the legendary king Arthur or tales of the Christianization of Europe. Historical time was, then, not continuous or linear in the way of diurnal time. Neither was yet another 'fictional' kind of time to which late medieval society accorded much value, that of eschatological time, counted through biblical ideas about the Apocalypse, the Day of Judgement, or visions of Purgatory or eternity (see Jacques le Goff, 1988: 13).

Accordingly, romance rarely clearly demarcates the division between real and imaginary places, or between past, present and future time. One of the effects of this, particularly for modern audiences, is a series of shifts or unsettling undercurrents operating below the surface narrative. For instance, trees or streams often border spaces or mark an entry point into a parallel dimension in romance. Often their mention in a story is the only clue to slippage from one to another. Sometimes a character will fall asleep or else be exiled, travelling vast distances and literally crossing borders. Wild open spaces and dense forests are often associated with magic and threat. Such spaces are liminal, as is the faery realm of romance and folklore in which conventional notions of time and space no longer hold and protagonists are subject to the forces of 'outside', beyond their control. In such a space of delay and deferral, anything might – and does – happen.

Space is then associated with transgression and/or transformation. Even enclosed, secret or private spaces like a lady's bedchamber, or an unknown tower or castle, can be dangerous, places where identities are simultaneously conferred *and* challenged. Romance often alerts us to the special nature of these places by juxtaposing inner and outer, or allying them to a structuring device such as an opposition between public and private. Other markers also cue its audiences. The inhabitants of romance's liminal, out-of-time other worlds are monsters, demons, hybrid beasts, faeries and women. These are the creatures marginalized in the real world for their shape-shifting, feminine perversions. They slip in and out, through insecure borders and thresholds, sometimes threatening and tricky, sometimes guiding, healing or answering riddles. Above all, their appearance in a narrative disrupts a real time-space continuum to offer, instead, transformation maybe and, more certainly, "a psychology of displacement" (Laskaya and Salisbury, 2001: 6).

For me, one of the most interesting examples of the subtle, yet far-reaching and disordering effects of romance's depiction of space is the story of *Sir Degaré*. At the start, inside and outside seem well delineated. There is the castle inhabited by Degaré's mother and grandfather, representing civilized society. Then there is Degaré's conception in a faery wood, an outlawed space of illicit desire that fractures structures crucial to social order: family, inheritance and succession, regulated sexuality. As the story continues, however, the border between what is real and unreal becomes increasingly porous and, so, exemplifies how Degaré's psychological crisis is ever more urgent. Equally, his grandfather's castle offers only an illusion of culture and restraint. The king of Brittany's excessive attachment to his daughter, Degaré's mother, ensures that she is effectively lost to normal society. The king defeats all potential suitors to keep her in the castle with him, thus thwarting any possibility of marriage and, consequently, the legitimate perpetuation of their family line.

From the beginning, then, an undercurrent of incestuous desire deforms this family script. With this in mind, the setting for Degaré's conception is less a simple opposition of inner/outer or order/disorder than it might initially appear. Though it places Degaré outside normative laws and, hence, is the impetus for his quest to discover his name and take up a position in society, it also symbolically enacts that society's deepest, unspoken desires. Degaré's mother is taken on a journey to visit her mother's grave hidden in the woods. Soon the retinue is lost. They sit for a while in the shade of a chestnut tree hoping to regain their bearings. Everyone, save Degaré's mother, falls asleep. The connotations of death and loss are, I think, obvious at this point. Degaré's mother wanders off on her own, gathering flowers and listening to bird song, seemingly eager to take advantage of her unexpected freedom and enjoy the natural setting after her virtual half-life in her father's castle (*Sir Degaré*, 63–71).

Yet all is not as it seems. The forest clearing is literally a lost space that echoes her castle confinement and stirs up mingled anxiety and desire. When Degaré's mother tries to return, she quickly discovers she cannot find her way. She is terrified wild beasts will eat her before any man can find her, that her own wild, natural side will encourage her to 'lose' herself, or her good name (79–88). At this precise moment, her demon lover appears. Degaré's father is both real and dreamed, a heterosexual fantasy of desire forever twisted out of shape by the shadow of the king's propensity for incest. Neither of Degaré's birth parents has a name – because both inhabit the realms of non-scriptible silence. In appearance and form, his father is the handsome knight the king refuses to allow his daughter to have. He is young, good-looking, "Gentil" or nobly born with an attractive, courteous manner; in fact, no man was "More apert [pleasing]" (97. See also 90–96). Seeking to allay the girl's fears, he claims to bring nothing but his sword, that – albeit damaged – phallus (mark of culture, language and masculine law) and chivalric symbol. He speaks, too, of his long-standing love *as though* he were a conventional suitor (98–105). When he makes plain his intention to have her with or without her consent, Degaré's mother tries to flee, but "nothing ne coude she do", and the knight rapes her (109). The entire scene is both nightmare and wish-fulfilment, the rape also symbolically displacing the threat of incest lurking inside the castle.

Degaré's conception, subsequent abandonment at birth and, later, his adoption by a hermit, all mark him as lost to symbolic, 'real' order or society. It is not until he defeats the king of Brittany and, inadvertently, marries his mother that he begins a long process of re-entry into proper space and time. Yet for most of that journey of self-discovery, Degaré slips further and further into a faery space that symbolizes his psychological limbo. Far from securing order, the wedding to his mother dramatizes the dysfunction at the heart of his family. Once more, incest is narrowly avoided, this time when Degaré remembers the 'Cinderella' gloves, left as part of his (unknown) patrimony, and his mother reveals her identity (725–29). Armed with half of his birth story, he can only complete it by returning to the actual place of his conception. So, he rides westwards, on into a kind of death, until, seemingly by chance, he reaches the same forest where his father raped his mother (725–29). Though Degaré travels miles each day he finds nothing. The place is empty of all recognized, real-life signs. There are no domestic beasts, only wild ones and birds singing on high until late in the evening (732–34). Like his mother before him, Degaré seems lost, unable to tell in which direction he is riding.

Each movement takes him a stage further on his journey and deeper into spaces of eerie displacement where he might be transformed. When he comes upon a river, he stands on the threshold of yet another boundary. Crossing it takes him to an island in the middle of the water. On that island is a castle, its bridge down and its gates wide, an open invitation to access. This enchanted castle mirrors the chivalric court he left behind at his grandfather's, and like that place it is full of lurking sexual violence. It is, too, a distorted image of the castle in Brittany, one that refracts and seeks to correct his grandfather's deformation of kinship bonds. Degaré's heritage is near-incest, heterosexual fantasy and rape combined. The enchanted castle, hidden in the ancient faery wood of his birthplace, threatens to repeat its illicit desires before pulling back and suppressing them. Although it seems empty, a welcoming fire blazes in the hearth and food is plentiful. Degaré's horse is fed while a manservant lays the table and lights torches. Degaré dines with a beautiful lady and her companions before following into her bedchamber. There he listens to music, drinks wine and sleeps.

The civilizing force of this castle is, though, an illusion, of sorts. Degaré is in a state of profound psychological distress at this point in the story, still without full knowledge of his origins and, hence, outside symbolic order. This displacement is enhanced by the magical, unearthly atmosphere of the place. Nothing is as it appears. The steward of the castle is a dwarf in the trappings of a man, with shoes like a knight's and a rich surcoat. The ladies who wait at table are armed with bows and arrows. The potential danger of the dwarf, sometime symbol of sexual depravity, and the active, aggression of the Amazonian style ladies, is well documented in medieval literature. Here, though, nothing ever quite happens, just as the double incest of his grandfather's castle – his own and his grandfather's – is neatly elided. Degaré falls into a trance-like state in this completely silent other-world, delays his quest for a moment longer (752–69).

In the morning the spell is partially broken. The lady speaks, at last, to berate him for his failure to protect her and her companions, before recounting the story of her family. She is the only child and heir of a rich baron (872–75). The most powerful knight in Brittany seeks to marry her and though she repeatedly refuses him, he hounds her, threatening abduction and killing so many of her protectors that there are no men left in the entire realm (888–903). Like Degaré, she too exists in a state of deferral, awaiting the inevitable and unable to act. Her story parallels that of Degaré's mother, for she will be taken whether she is willing or not (903), and her suitor has also thwarted her chances of marrying elsewhere. In order to repair this double dysfunction, Degaré must kill the lady's assailant and undo the threat of rape. In some senses, he has already done this. Although he spent the night in the lady's chamber, asleep and spellbound, he had no sexual potency. It is not until he wins the battle for her hand that he is able to follow her into the bedroom and take up her sexual invitation. Once this is done, and he agrees to return within the year, the lady arms him, gives him gold and horses and sends him on the final stage of his quest (59–83). And there, in the same forest, he at last meets his faery father, reclaims the lady and reunites his birth parents (1029–62). *Sir Degaré* seeks to re-inscribe a heterosexual family script. Its distortion of space and time, both embodies the psychological trauma produced by illicit desire *and* resolves it through the sanctity of marriage. In so doing, however, it takes the reader so far into the liminal, highly pleasurable spaces the narrative invokes that those same spaces come to seem more, not less, real.

Sir Orfeo similarly disturbs with its too-neat resolution and imposition of an order that seems far less resonant than the liminal gaps it leaves behind. The poem's echoing of the classical Orpheus and Euridyce myth might, in some measure, account for its repeated allusions to death. When Herodis learns she must depart with the faery king, she rends her clothes, weeps, screams and tears at herself in gestures akin to ritual mourning (*Sir Orfeo*, 53–58). Likewise, Orfeo's ten-year retreat into a wilderness where he sees and speaks to no one, suggests his profound sense of loss and grief for his beloved wife. The world of faery, found deep in the bowels of the earth and extravagantly and artificially lit up, depicts a kind of hell. Yet the symbolic deaths the story foregrounds perhaps allude more forcefully to its central theme, which, I suggest, is the failure of dynasty.

When Orfeo glimpses his wife in the realm of faery just before she disappears into the underworld, he wishes that he too was dead (307–14). This moment completes the refusal of his proper place as king and dynastic head. Early on, Orfeo renounces his kingdom to head for a death-in-life abjection where he seems to accept that his queen has gone forever. He stops searching for her and, instead, passively waits in a suspension of time that mirrors the dreamy, frozen-in-death tableau that he finds in the court of the faery king. During his time in the wilderness, Orfeo's only activity is playing the harp; even then the creatures he charms with his music sit immobile as soon as he stops playing (279–80). These images of stasis intersect Orfeo's abdication of his kingship. He leaves that world in the hands of the same trusted steward who later thinks him dead (204–18). The steward's lengthy tenure as king implicitly contrasts Orfeo's lack of active care of his people. Even Orfeo's army fails to prevent Herodis's abduction by a stronger, seemingly more chivalric king: though a thousand knights stand guard, she is spirited away right from under their noses (167–70).

Images of death-like sleep and a sense of endless waiting permeate the text. Herodis wanders into an orchard in full bloom one May morning. The intimations of hope and vitality in this space soon fade. Herodis and Orfeo are childless, a fact borne out by the steward's surrogate kingship and later succession. Herodis sits under a tree and falls asleep for the entire day. She dreams of a faery lover who, like those faeries in other romance tales, vows to take her regardless of her own desires (33–48). We know little of Orfeo's kingdom but that textual silence allows for the fuller scripting of a faery world, which suddenly seems more legible and real than actuality. In Orfeo's world, there is no guarantee of order, not in day-to-day military protection and not for the future which, without children, cannot be assured. This lack of order is conveyed, too, by Herodis's easy loss and Orfeo's renunciation of the crown. The faery king's realm de-familiarizes this temporal reality. It is splendid, full of might and activity. Herodis dreams of armed knights, magnificent castles, towers, rivers, woodlands and a king who promises to abduct her (109–50). Equally, in a parallel vision of otherness perceived by Orfeo in snatches at the edges of his mind's eye, there is hunting, dancing, minstrelsy, ladies hawking, a world of pleasure all safely bounded by a thousand armed knights, swords drawn and at the ready (257–89).

Later, though, that faery dimension is twisted out of shape in a manoeuvre that parallels the restoration of real-world order. Orfeo suddenly becomes active again. He scurries through rock after a vanishing Herodis and descends into the faery court. He arrives at an inverted, unnatural paradise, to a huge, crenellated castle bolstered by shining, gem-encrusted pillars that blaze night and day in a deformation of real, natural time (325–52). Inside is a vision of eternal death. Scores of people are suspended at the moment of their demise or else posed in attitudes of violence. Some are wounded, some strangled as they eat or else bound, drowned, shrivelled, insane. Others are dying in childbirth or like Herodis who is caught asleep under the unnatural imp-tree (363–84). Descent to the underworld is a classic romance motif that usually signals regeneration and reparation. Accordingly, Orfeo's harp music enables him to return with Herodis and re-enter his own world.

Still in his wilderness 'disguise', he tells his steward how he took the harp from a dead man torn to pieces by wild animals (535–46). This detail echoes the faery king's threat to dismember Herodis if she refuses to surrender to him (169–74), a threat she replicates in part when she tears at her own body in distress (106–06). In the context of the poem's discussion of what constitutes proper kingship, it is a telling one. The medieval world imaged what we might loosely term the nation state as a proper – that is whole and intact – body with the king as its head. Though Orfeo's steward presumably keeps the realm securely in check, when Orfeo steps away from his social responsibilities as king, he leaves his subjects exposed to potential disorder and a violation instanced in these details of bodily disaggregation, as well as in Herodis's loss to a rival king. In part, order is already threatened as I suggested earlier in Orfeo's failure to produce a legitimate son and heir.

Sir Orfeo's insistence upon loss and death also cross-connects the well-known and highly conflicted myth of Orpheus recounted in Virgil, Ovid, Horace and medieval writers like Boethius, Nicholas Trivet, Boccaccio and Christine de Pizan. There Orpheus's wonderful harp playing gains him entry to the underworld and restores to life Eurydice. He loses her forever when he disobeys the god of death's command never to look back as he leads her up into the light. In *Sir Orfeo* it seems that civilization and culture are restored when Orfeo's music breaks the charm that holds the faery palace in thrall and defeats the faery king when, previously, his army could not. Yet the cumulative effect of the tale's liminal spaces is to distort taken-for-granted assumptions and hollow out any simplistic notion of order, especially when its borders so easily slip. On his return to a temporal dimension, Orfeo's experiences have so physically altered him that his steward does not know who he is (210–44). Even outside the space of the immediate story, those other versions of the Orfeo/Orpheus myth continue to resonate with their connotations of failure, stasis and loss (see Sturges, 2001: 109–22); they may well have the last word on this Middle English poem too.

INSIDE/OUT

Sir Gawain and the Green Knight deploys space and time to particularly subtle effect as part of its wider, profoundly unsettling ambivalences. Gawain passes through real places – North Wales, the Wirral, Anglesey. Scholars suggest that even the Green Chapel is an actual, natural feature of the north-west midlands landscape from where the poet writes, although its exact location continues to be disputed. This geography corresponds to the real time punctuating the action. The Arthurian court is challenged during Yuletide. Gawain has a year and a day to rendezvous for a repeat encounter with the Green Knight on New Year's Day. The poem holds events in a time frame that comprises religious festivals and specific calendar dates: All Saints' Day, Christmas Eve, Christmas Day, St John's Day, New Year's Day and the Feast of Circumcision. As well as this measurable time, it invokes a cycle of decay and regeneration by noting the passing of the seasons. This natural framework melds with a cosmic time revealed via Christian allusions.

This reality is also set against imagined spaces like the forests through which Gawain passes and his journey across a wilderness (the Cheshire plain?) where he faces wolves, wild animals and more mythical creatures like trolls, giants, dragons and the 'wodwo' or Wild-Men of the woods (*Sir Gawain and the Green Knight*, 720–24). Here in the compressed space of several lines, Gawain's battles are quickly glossed, as if unreal while in a similar space–time distortion Hautdesert rises as if from nowhere. This is the fairy-tale castle described in great detail as though it is real, even as it is compared to a paper cut-out, thus heightening its illusory qualities, and no one seems ever to have heard of it (703–08, 795–802). When Bertilak returns there at the end of the poem, it is as if he disappears into the realm of myth or magic for he goes "Whider-warde-so-ever he wolde" – wherever he wants, wherever that might be (2478). Hautdesert is, at one and the same time, the double of Camelot, a civilized space upheld by Bertilak, *and* an enchanted place ruled by the Green Knight.

Its obverse, the outside space of the Green Chapel, is especially isolated and wild, a threatening spot said to belong to the devil (2180–96). Guarded by rocks and a stream, it is, too, the setting for an intensely private one-to-one encounter that up-ends the highly theatrical display of the previous meeting between Gawain and the Green Knight. Its precise nature always eludes us. Does the Green Chapel's enclosure suggest a womb-like space in which to enact a re-birth or to renegotiate identities? Is it an ancient death barrow where Gawain, symbolically at least, faces his own death?

The juxtaposition of inside and outside seen throughout intersects other binaries – public/private, masculine/feminine, order/disorder – to tell something of the conflicted nature of meaning in this complex poem. It is perhaps self-evident to remark how the court or great hall represents civilized, contained, masculine space. Yet inside the castle are other more intimate, tighter spaces like bedchambers, enclosed as miniatures within that same masculine order and adding their own extra dimension. So, too, because borders rarely hold in *Sir Gawain and the Green Knight*, 'inside' and 'outside' continually shift.

Arthur's court seems to sign itself as a safely delineated space of public order and guaranteed privilege. The opening scene of the poem depicts it as a place of revelry. Camelot is in full swing of the 15-day long festivities of Yuletide, with tournaments, dancing, feasts, singing, games and exchange of gifts. Many small details confirm the impression that this is a lavish, even extravagant – and, so, successful – court. Guinevere sits on a luxurious dais (707) for example, and the New Year's Day feast has silver platters full of food (116–29) at a time when outside, as Gawain will soon learn, there is privation with birds dying of hunger and cold (747). The narrator emphasizes the youth of this court and, by implication, its idealism or innocence. Arthur is young, handsome and fun-loving (53–57). He is said to be restless, refusing to eat on feast days until he has seen a joust or heard an adventurous tale (90–99). The date, January the 1st, contributes to this sense of glorious potential, for this is the new year of a court in its "first age" (54), full of high spirits and untainted, as yet, by the adultery and treason to come in the Arthurian legend.

For come it will, in full accordance with historical time. This is, then, not quite the safely delineated space it might appear to be. It is a juvenile, faintly reckless court where Arthur is described as "childgered [boyish]" (86) and even "brayn wylde" (89) to connote irresponsibility. Equally, his appetite for high jinks and diversion means that the Green Knight steps with ease over the threshold of this court and 'outside' readily contaminates 'inside'. The narrator implies that the Green Knight's entry is Arthur's fault when he writes "for [because]" he wants to be excited by brave talk (492). Here 'inside' and 'order' are in the process of negotiation and not secured safely at the height of Arthur's idyllic, so-called, reign. This air of vulnerability gains additional resonance once we realize that Morgan is responsible for the Green Knight's threatening intrusion and the spring for Gawain's adventures. To view this opening scene retrospectively – in other words, from a distorting historical perspective – opens it up to disorder and queers our understanding of the whole poem. Concepts that seem secure or familiar are challenged and re-rehearsed once we accept that Morgan is the catalyst for a series of cross-connections that disturb the surface order of the text.

ENGENDERING IDENTITIES

Earlier, I suggested that the narrator of Chaucer's *Man of Law's Tale* attempts to impose a particular narrative frame upon a story that ultimately fails to hold it in place. The Man of Law's portrayal of Custance is a perfect illustration of an exemplary femininity, which was esteemed in late medieval theological and patristic texts, as well as in literature and other discursive expositions. In such instances, attributes of femininity were modelled on the female body. This body was read as an open, material entity. Its orifices rendered it especially corrupt or potentially sinful for they permitted both penetration and leakage, whether bodily emissions or non-scriptible sound. That paradigmatic body was also associated with oral excess, was appetitive and sexually voracious, allegedly. As such, women had to work especially hard to overcome these so-called, natural tendencies. They were thus advised to moderate speech, dress and behaviour, to exercise the kind of restraint and decorum supposedly apparent in the Virgin Mary whose miraculous virgin birth perfectly exemplifies bodily closure.

The Man of Law tries to present Custance as a passive victim, merely an instrument of God and ready to enact the will of fathers both heavenly and real. Her near-saintly perfection corresponds to the merchant's oral remarks about her virtues. There are direct references to her as holy (*Man of Law's Tale*, 692, 721, 1149). We hear about her prayers to God and of many biblical miracles or divine intervention (449–505, 511, 617, 923–45, 950–52). So, too, he stresses the pathos of her situation. She is a "sely innocent" (682) who incites compassion in all who meet her, while the narrator's increasingly vehement apostrophes work to appropriate a figure who is, in part, a mere cipher: "O my Custance" he cries (803) or "Allas! Custance, thou hast no champioun!" (631). Romance often seems to deride female agency, unless it is a virtuous feminine pastime such as embroidery or child care. Similarly, as an empty sign, many romance women have no name or are the archetypal 'Lady', pivotal to the plot but otherwise merely emblematic. In *Sir Gawain and the Green Knight*, Guinevere represents the glory of an Arthurian order. As such, she is silent and static, a trophy to be coveted or won. She sits on a high dais as befits her rank but also in order to display her iconic significance. The poem offers little in the way of specifics; we simply know that she is the loveliest of all, a renown underscored by the fine silks and valued Toulouse fabric decorating her seat (74–84).

Yet, as ever in romance stories, traditional depictions rarely connote everything there is to know about gender. The same robe that in conventional readings turns Emaré into an object of exchange, for instance, also allows her to step into the subject position of the narrative as the title of the poem suggests, to become both the masculine 'hero' *and* the object of her own story. Equally, feminine qualities might also denote transgression, calling to mind the active and resourceful heroines of classical tales. In the *Man of Law's Tale*, Custance converts Hermengyld and others to enlarge and reinforce a Christian community in Northumberland at a time when the faith is outlawed (*Man of Law's Tale*, 533–74). Similarly, though the Man of Law insists she overcomes attempted rape thanks to the intercession of the Virgin Mary, her active struggling tips her assailant overboard (920–24). Both Custance and Emaré hide behind a feminine mask of silence to conceal their origins, and while Emaré is 'driven' by the sea, Chaucer's version more clearly suggests direct agency when "She dryveth forth" (505) and "in the see she dryveth forth hir weye" (875). Even as romance's grotesque old hags and sexually promiscuous women comply with antifeminist tradition, *at the same time* they undo the apparent oppositions they seemingly embed. Such women are often associated with magic, are keepers of secrets or mischief makers who point up a feminine potential for havoc even as they double as enchanted or bewitched heroines.

Guinevere's portrayal in the youthful court of *Sir Gawain and the Green Knight* is unexpected, seemingly unmarked by her more usual notoriety as promiscuous and, thus, a catalyst for the collapse of Arthurian ideals. She is, though, but one of a series of images that cross-cut and interconnect in the poem and which speak to the central instability of constructions of gender. The figure of Guinevere is doubled in the Lady who, in turn, finds an inverted reflection in the old woman (Morgan) accompanying her. At first sight, this latter pairing calls up the dual notion of womanhood I remarked a little earlier. The nameless Lady is, like Guinevere, an object to be looked at. In contrast to her companion, the old crone, she is fresh and youthful. The text invites close-up scrutiny of her uncovered face, shoulders, throat and breasts (*Sir Gawain and the Green Knight*, 950–55, 1736–41). Unlike the woman who flanks her, the Lady is said to be the loveliest to taste. The other one is short and dumpy with low-hanging buttocks, the perfect foil to the Lady's beauty (986–89). The disguised Morgan is veiled, wrapped in neckerchiefs and muffled in a silk turban so that we glimpse her only in bits and pieces – her lips, eyes, nose, brow, and ruddy, wrinkled complexion; in short, she is "soure to se" (952–64).

Yet this version of Morgan is much more than the simple opposite of the Lady who is also in a triangular relationship with Guinevere. The Lady, says the narrator, surpasses Guinevere in every way (945). Not only is she more beautiful, she is also more active, an attribute that undercuts her exemplary femininity by associating her with masculine action; of course, it also allies her to feminine subversion – not least through the revelation that she is Morgan's puppet. In tracing the Lady's all-out attempt to seduce Gawain, the poem both negates an emblematic ideal witnessed here in Guinevere *and* displaces Guinevere's reputation for sexual promiscuity connoted in other Arthurian tales. The Lady enters Gawain's bedroom early one morning, unannounced and uninvited. She locks the door behind her and positions herself above him in a literal, woman-on-top manoeuvre vilified in medieval thinking as a feminine perversion (1233). She pins Gawain down, placing her arms either side of him and refusing to let him get up now that she has him caught (1223–25). The Lady calls him by his name in masculine-style appropriation, and teasingly challenges his reputation for courtesy and honour in the service of love (1208, 1226–29, 1273–76, 1480–84, 1508–29). At the feast and in full view of everyone in the court, including her husband, she steals side-long glances at Gawain (1658–63) to compromise him, just as previously *she* took *him* in her arms and kissed him (1505).

As ever in *Sir Gawain and the Green Knight*, what is actually visualized is far from being a singular reality. The old crone chaperoning the Lady is her antifeminist double *and* Morgan le Fay. Morgan's physical description keeps her out of the circulation of desire set up in the poem while, thanks to all those coverings, she is never fully visible. Thus she evades full representation and, in so doing, slips between categories to unlace them all. Long past youth, she lacks even the limited power as a woman conferred by beauty. Yet, later, when he reveals her supernatural agency, Bertilak terms her a goddess so potent she could make anyone "ful tame". He tells, too, how Morgan instigates every event and transformation – including his own. This deceptively casual aside is signalled early on when Morgan and Bertilak sit adjacent to each other on elevated seats of honour in the hall (1000–03). Equally, the narrator highlights Morgan's pivotal role when he tracks Gawain's genealogy through a female line in which she is central: as Gawain's aunt, as Arthur's half-sister, and as the *daughter* of the *duchess* of Tintagel (2664–65, emphasis mine). In spite of Morgan's non-scriptible representation, she – not the protagonists of the story's title – impels the plot in *Sir Gawain and the Green Knight*. This transgression – intimated when, for instance, she leads the Lady by the hand (947) – provokes a set of 'perversions' which accumulate to unsettle audiences and to call into question hetero-normative 'rules.'

PROBLEMATISING DIFFERENCE

One of the unwritten expectations of a heterosexual paradigm is that gender and sexuality are predicated on the notion of difference. Same-sex desire is immediately foreclosed while repeated and oppositional performances of gender seemingly embed sexual difference as natural or given. Since most romances involve marriage and a classic love triangle in which the hero successfully fights for his lady, we might anticipate that the romance genre more than any other underwrites such thinking. Though *Sir Gawain and the Green Knight* is not the only story in which conventional assumptions unravel, it perhaps offers the perfect example.

The confrontation between Gawain and the Green Knight problematizes sexual difference. Romance's conventional *gigantomachia* – where the hero battles with a monster or hybrid creature – is contorted by the Green Knight's bodily inflation. In *Of Giants* (1999), Cohen theorizes the giant's body as one where everything that might gender it as securely masculine fails to hold. A knight's encounter with such a body is, therefore, crucial, a battle which attempts to play out and fix masculinity. In turn, a 'guaranteed' masculinity helps to shore up social (chivalric) order (Cohen, 1999: 68–69, 96–116). The fact that the Green Knight is no ordinary monster renders this simple romance formula entirely suspect. The Green Knight is a super-sized man, a femininized – because supernatural – conundrum, *and* a real knight, Bertilak, the urbane host of Hautdesert. As such, the context of Gawain's so-called coming-of-age battle is exceptionally diffuse and conflicted.

The relationship between Gawain and Bertilak is simultaneously homosocial – one of the means by which masculinity is produced – *and* implicitly homosexual. The two of them affirm masculine, chivalric bonds when they feast and drink together or propose an Exchange of Winnings, a pact sealed with a drink and a 'social' kiss (*Sir Gawain and the Green Knight*, 1112, 1118). Other details also support the natural workings of chivalry: for instance, their private conversations or Bertilak's invitations to stay and not ride to the Green Chapel (1029–34, 1042, 1068). At the same time, these somewhat isolated examples accumulate to draw together a web of correspondences and affinities, which subtly alter the dynamics of their masculine relationship. When they sit and talk away from the speculative gaze of the court (1664–82), the scene parallels those between the Lady and Gawain in the privacy of his bedchamber. There, under the guise of chivalric banter and word-play, the Lady, too, entices Gawain to linger and take his pleasure with her in bed.

If the Lady's actions are seductive, Bertilak's are rather more coercive. He insists that Gawain stays late in bed while the other men go out hunting (1069–76, 1071–72, 1096–99, 1676). On occasions, he touches or holds him, makes him sit with him or orchestrates Gawain's movements with gentle, physical pressure, just as the Lady jokingly pins him to the bed (1029, 1083). Gawain becomes increasingly passive in this strange castle. The kisses Gawain exchanges with Bertilak as part of their pact also invert the Lady's attempts at seduction. Each time, Bertilak offers up the spoils of the day's hunting and then waits for something in return. This exchange is a public spectacle performed in full view of the court, unlike the scenes in Gawain's private room. On the first occasion, Gawain passes on the Lady's kiss, as courteously as he is able (1389). On the second, he presents two kisses, still social kisses but now offered with his hands clasped behind Bertilak's head in a parody of a heterosexual embrace (1629–40). The third time, Gawain approaches Bertilak and kisses him three times "As saverly and sadly as he hem sette couthe" (1937): that is, with feeling, firmly.

Part of the escalating queer resonance of these kisses stems from the parallel exchange between Gawain and Bertilak's alter-ego, the Green Knight. During their first encounter at Arthur's court, Gawain is active and dominant, literally positioned above the Green Knight who lies prostrate upon the floor. The Green Knight sweeps up his long hair to expose the white nape of his neck in preparation for Gawain's blow (417–28). Gawain chops off his head with a single blow in a clear signalling of masculine performance. The Green Knight's exposure of skin and flesh is more than a simple submission, however. Rather, it parodies the Lady's sexual, feminine provocation; our first sight of her takes in her fleshly display and fine figure, her bare white neck and throat (933–34, 1740–41). When the Exchange of Blows is repeated, Gawain meets his adversary in an enclosed space well away from prying eyes, just as he did with the Lady in his private room. Gawain submits, his head forward and neck exposed, ready for a blow that gently nicks the skin, leaving a small hole and spilling blood in a perverse 'kiss' or quasi-penetration (2256). Once more, the encounter has an erotic charge. The economical description is bereft of the graphic detail of other romance fights with their repeated thrusts and phallic blades sinking to the hilt (see *Sir Degaré* and *Sir Gowther*), a traditional discourse that, ironically, de-sexualizes these acts. Instead, it focuses the moment and adds to its unsettling thrill.

It is not only the Exchange of Blows-Exchange of Winnings sequence that exerts a queer force over *Sir Gawain and the Green Knight*. The Lady's assays on Gawain's body are made with the full knowledge of her husband, a fact that Bertilak later admits (2358–63). This perverse triangular dynamic apes normative heterosexual triangles in which the hero battles it out with a monster or a rival to achieve full masculine subjectivity. Here, in *Sir Gawain and the Green Knight*, a strange telescoping lens distorts conventional paradigms. The Lady is already married, to Gawain's host and chivalric bondsman Bertilak, who is also the 'monster' Gawain faces in the Green

Chapel and the seeming instigator of the whole plot. The erotic potential of Bertilak's voyeurism gains added force from a similar scene in *Sir Gawain and the Carl of Carlisle*. There, like Bertilak, the Carl seats Gawain next to his beautiful wife to encourage a desire for which he later admonishes his guest. In the bedroom, the Carl and his wife both help Gawain to undress. The wife kisses Gawain in full sight of her husband, presses him ever further to arouse him while the Carl watches. The scene ends when the Carl insists Gawain stops before he goes too far; he later offers to marry him to his daughter instead, thus seemingly channelling disordering and illicit desire (*Sir Gawain and the Carl of Carlisle*, 439–95). The poem manages to make explicit, however, some of the more disturbing aspects of *Sir Gawain and the Green Knight*, which gather even more strength once we recall that Morgan, and not Bertilak, drives the plot.

This is undoubtedly the queerest twist of all. Morgan's desire to 'touch' Guinevere by frightening her to death – the reason she sends the Green Knight to disturb the Yuletide festivities – is manifested in the way she employs Bertilak and his wife to manipulate Gawain. Gawain's body, tested by his hosts in all their guises, becomes part of a choreography in which he is a conduit of desire. His family relationship to Guinevere and to Morgan means that he is a pivotal link in their dynamics. When the Lady, Bertilak and the Green Knight physically or implicitly touch Gawain they also make contact with Guinevere via a series of displacements. Ultimately, Morgan does not succeed in so terrorizing Guinevere that she dies, but neither are the sodomitical tendencies of the tale recuperated for heterosexuality and social order, as many critics – even queer theorists – maintain. After the skewed *gigantomachia* in *Sir Gawain and the Green Knight*, Gawain does not win the girl. Neither does he stamp any authority on the Arthurian court. Instead, everyone laughs at his explanation of events and re-signs the baldric as a badge of honour, thereby suppressing its more nuanced readings. Gawain rides out alone, away from the company of his fellow knights, aimlessly roaming without a quest, and without a love object. Order is not neatly secured. Rather, *Sir Gawain and the Green* Knight *re-orders* its masculine world, subtly shifts its parameters and, thus, leaves us with a fundamental disquiet that we cannot fully absorb.

Sir Launfal is a similarly troubling poem. Just as the homosocial world of chivalry is bolstered by repeated external display, the story of *Sir Launfal* turns on a visible-invisible 'proof' of masculinity.

Launfal's chivalric reputation is conflicted from the moment Guinevere publicly insults him by passing him over in the gift-giving ceremony that marks her marriage to Arthur. Her action is never explained. Rather, it remains an implicit part of her alleged predilection for disruptive behaviour. Its effect is to suggest that though the rest of the court esteems Launfal he is, in some way, not a worthy Round Table knight, not, in short, a man. As a result, Launfal has to over-perform both as a warrior and a lover if he is to refute this slur upon his character. Thus Launfal's battle with the fearsome Sir Valentine – pun intended? – is designed to secure his name. Sir Valentine's challenge is to prove his love for Tryamour and to prove his masculinity (*Sir Launfal*, 523–28). Is Sir Valentine here suggesting that Launfal is, as yet, simply untested as a knight? Or that he is homosexual? Above all, the wording of the challenge demonstrates the extent to which masculinity is founded on sexual difference and clear oppositions. Accordingly, Launfal offers a display of exceptional violence, during which he kills Sir Valentine and many others (601–10). The scene is then doubled in a heterosexual and verbal 'exchange of blows' with Guinevere. Here Launfal is seemingly defeated by Guinevere's public outing of his perceived and ambiguous sexuality. She jeers "Thou lovist no woman ne no woman the" (689). Even though Launfal declares his love for the invisible fairy queen Tryamour, there is continued and ambiguous reference to the word 'bachelor' (691–99). Launfal himself repeats Guinevere's words when he tells Arthur that she said "I nas no man" and seek "Ne no womannes companie" (775–77).

Since both chivalry and, in theoretical terms, gender adhere through repetition, these doublings accrete to further embed a certain ambiguity about whom or what Launfal is. If the charge against Launfal came solely from a spiteful Guinevere then its force might be negligible. Yet it is repeated by Sir Valentine, made public by Launfal and also gains bizarre credence in the world of faery. The description of Tryamour and her court is pure heterosexual fantasy. A band of exotic maidens take Launfal to their queen who reclines on a canopied bed, clothes unbuttoned almost to the waist because of the heat (277–300). Having demanded his presence, this semi-naked beauty declares undying love, invites him into her bed and promises to restore his credentials as a knight (315–66). All of Launfal's wishes come true at once. Later, when Guinevere and even his fellow knights demand visible proof of his beloved's existence, impossibly she comes to his rescue to appear before them all as one even lovelier than Guinevere (913–24).

Yet this tangible evidence of Launfal's heterosexual, masculine identity is an illusion. In faery, Launfal is completely femininized. He sits in the shade of a tree, having fled from the gaze of his own world. He is passive, allowing faeries to abduct him and take him away (220–48) in a scene oddly reminiscent of those faery rapes common to other romances. Here a woman 'rapes' a man, keeps him in a female-dominated, fantasy world replete with images of extravagance and otherness. Tryamour and her subjects are exoticized, dressed in Indian silks, studded with Indian gems, and sitting in opulent, pitched pavilions fabricated by Saracens, in a place said to outdo anything at Arthur's court or Alexander the Great's palace (220–48, 266, 275–86, 883–91, 931–72). Launfal is entertained, softened up and given material aid he might only dream of. Even on the battlefield, magical assistance compromises his masculine and chivalric prowess (577–600) and, again, when at the end Tryamour rides out to him as though he is a damsel in distress. Launfal disappears into faery, returning each year like a ghost to taunt the Arthurian court in a performance of chivalry he lacked in the real world (1024–38).

Failure is not confined to Launfal. A masculine chivalric order fails to regulate itself when it allows Guinevere to shame Launfal – who is, after all, Arthur's long-serving steward – and when it is unable to protect Arthur from the scandal to come in other Arthurian story-cycles. Neither can that world secure its 'name', just as Launfal cannot guarantee his, for faery visibly ruptures it. Above all, the queer circuit of exchange in *Sir Launfal* is not based upon the distant possibility of same-sex desire amongst men. Instead, a perverse feminine drives both the faery world and the real. In the latter, Guinevere's desires overwrite sworn, homosocial loyalties to disorder the court. In faery, Tryamour desires and actively manipulates Launfal through whom she is able to burst into visibility and 'touch' Guinevere in real time and space. The rivalry between the two women is established from the moment Launfal speaks Tryamour's name and declares her more beautiful than Guinevere (694–99) – just as the faery palace outdoes anything seen at Camelot. Guinevere insists that Arthur defend her honour but loses with his superlative assessment of Tryamour's loveliness (913–24). In a moment unique to the Middle English version of *Sir Launfal*, Tyramour then breathes on Guinevere. This literal queer touch blinds her, thus refuting a masculine world order based on sight or tangible experience and replacing it with an invisible, unruly impulse that holds over and above the real (1006–08).

What are we to make of this resonant detail? Does the faery realm remind us that masculine order is always only secured through the expulsion of feminine perversions that are prior to it and which continually threaten its borders? Does it tell of the dissatisfactions of chivalry or speak to contemporaneous civil strife? Or is this a poem about gender, one that uses the device of chivalry to call into question those norms that structure western symbolic order? Certainly, the Launfal-Tryamour pairing fails to convince or to guarantee heterosexuality, not least because it is forever invisible and, hence, illegible to the real world.

ENGENDERING NATIONS

Earlier I began to explore theories about space and time as gendered entities. The notion of space as feminine arises from a sense of it as bounded or contained, a domesticated, colonized space. Alternatively, space may be feminine by virtue of it being wild or dangerous and unruly. In contrast, a number of scholars view time as masculine for it is proper (finite and measurable), linear and progressive. Time is, too, integral to a masculine symbolic order; that is, the psychic or figurative space where we name and, thus, configure the known, real world. This world is composed of the moment of verbal communication and exchanged as such in real or temporal time. However, this binary division is not as secure as it might seem. As well as the problematic of historical time – which I discussed earlier – temporal or masculine time is always cross-cut by two different kinds of feminine time. Cyclic time consists of recurrent, biological rhythms such as gestation, while monumental or eternal time refers to any inexplicable, out-of-time moment – including *jouissance* (joy) or ecstasy (see Part Two: Reading and Research). Space and time, thus, both produce ambivalences and difficulties that speak to the anxieties about the ways in which we construct social and national order.

Before I move on to discuss what is, probably, the best example of these conflicted notions in medieval romance, I wish to draw together some other aspects of my ongoing discussion of romance texts. I have already highlighted how one of the founding myths of western culture is a story of origins witnessed in family kinship patterns.

These stories help to embed individual subjectivities by reminding us of who we are and how we come to be. They are also part of the historical past of communities and nations; as such, they draw peoples together, help to define and police borders of all kinds, gender included, and feed into concepts of social and national stability. Such scripts always stress heterosexual paradigms and seek to regulate desire by expelling unsettling same-sex affinities, sodomitical activities – whatever these might be – and monstrous or miscegenated offspring. A case in point is the Albina myth said to define the founding of Britain. Here Brutus defeats a race of half-giants spawned by the abandoned Albina princesses and so colonizes the land to 'claim' Britain.

Thus theories of gender and sexuality, together with psychoanalytical and postcolonial literary theory, interconnect to help us think through medieval romance texts. One way these critical tools might come together is in a discussion of queer time and space. To queer time and/or space is to keep them on the move, an unsettling enterprise that ensures such concepts – as well as any other ideas they intersect – are always in process; instead of helping to confer identities, queer time or space points up contingent yet-to-be-fixed eddies and swirls. Above all, rather than being a story of origins, 'queer' is more interested in that story's more conflicted elements, in its displacements, paradoxes, and correspondences.

Emaré and the *Man of Law's Tale* both plot the co-ordinates of a temporal journey made in real time. Emaré travels from the place of her birth to Wales, from Wales to Rome and back, knitting up, finally, the complex family relations to which she is central. Custance also tracks a series of geographical points: Rome to Syria to Northumberland, back to Northumberland and then, at last, home again to Rome. We see, too, how she passes through the narrow strait between Gibraltar and Morocco, for example. Her European journey in particular finds added resonance in chronicle stories which tell of the Christianization of Europe achieved by her real-life counterpart and her son, the Roman Emperor Mauricius. Equally, reference to specific points is part of a broader attempt by the Man of Law to fix Custance in place. Her trip from Rome to Syria is an exogamy designed to achieve the surety of her as a wife *and* as a colonizing Christian power. Those same co-ordinates domesticate both Custance and Emaré by labelling them: 'daughter', 'wife', 'mother'. Equally, as I have already suggested, they are both held in a framework of exemplary femininity. These traceable, 'fixed' points of the narrative hold, too, what is essentially the same story in cyclic time. Both women give birth and both follow repeated cycles of arrival and exile. Custance, for instance, is said to sit and wait inside Alla's castle, biding her time in a cyclic limbo throughout the duration of her pregnancy (*Man of Law's Tale*, 720–22).

Perhaps the most memorable part of this tale is its queerly distorted exiles. The story's temporal co-ordinates exist alongside the ocean journeys where a woman floats in a rudderless boat, randomly criss-crossing the globe. These journeys detract from any sense of a map that is fixed, despite the named places. Rather, each arrival is less an end-point than a temporary, even accidental, arrest, part of a constant movement that keeps its protagonists on the literal edges of time and space. Custance arrives in Northumberland only when her ship is grounded on the shore by the tide (508–10). Later in the story, she is cast up near a heathen castle from whose vantage point everyone stands and stares at her (904–17). Adrift on the open sea, by chance her uncle finds her and takes her back to Rome (967–75). Exile is a free-floating space, out of time or else in eternal time. Time is elided in the vastness of the ocean: Custance drifts for years and days (463) and, again, five years or more (901), her ship tossed here and there (945–48) in an in-between seascape.

In this queer black hole, Custance and Emaré are homeless, nameless, beyond kin, outside language and culture and in a silence only occasionally filled by the Man of Law who ventriloquizes Custance's thoughts. So too, the inexorable rhythm of their movement defies logic. They arrive, depart, and repeat the cycle. Though we can map *some* movement, on the whole their motion seems aimless. Thus the repetition of 'driven' implies motion without agency or control, so that Emaré is 'driven' from wave to wave by wind and rain, or caught in a storm that propels her towards Rome (*Emaré*, 315, 322, 331, 337, 679). Custance is also 'driven', sometimes west, sometimes north and south, sometimes east (*Man of Law's Tale*, 947–49). In this psychic space and time, everything is suspended or occluded in contrast to the women's more active participation in daily life. Above all, these same plot-points of arrival–departure, marriage–birth–exile open up queer spaces, which distort received patterns of kinship and shatter the main narrative frame, in the *Man of Law's Tale* especially. Each fixed marker sparks a crisis of identification: who or what is this woman? Where is she leaving from and why? Where is she going? In this way, the tale reworks connections and alliances to make us rethink accepted notions of time and space, and, in addition, definitions of collective identity.

These crises are not just personal but national, something witnessed in the anxiety about assimilation Custance and Emaré each incite in, for example, their respective mothers-in-law. Custance and Emaré inhabit the subject position of 'stranger' or 'foreigner'. The impetus for this out-of-law, non-scriptible state is incest, in both cases, despite the Man of Law's vehement protestations to the contrary. Custance's exogamy is the legitimate way to contain an incest taboo that is the touchstone of western civilization. She is sent off to a "strange" and "Barbre" nation (268 and 281) where she is received as a "creature" (463, 694) and an "elf" (744). This terminology calls attention to her status as an outsider, one who is beyond cultural understanding or frame of reference. This state is further embedded when she refuses to tell of her origins or else speaks in a version of her own mother-tongue, something she does while in Northumberland (516). Custance's difference is also flagged when, in an attempt to invoke his audiences' compassion during her trial for murder, the Man of Law notes her pale face in the crowd (645–51). Custance is even physically unlike the people with whom she lives. Her apparent ethnic difference is corroborated when Alla and her father both recognize her distinctive face in Maurice, the future heir of Northumberland and Rome (1030–36, 1053–54, 1063, 1096). Emaré also conceals her origins and takes the name of Egaré, meaning 'outcast'. She too is repeatedly defined by her seeming difference, something enhanced by the robe she persists in wearing and which makes her seem outlandish. As a result, her future mother-in-law advises against the marriage, calling her 'fiendish': that is, one not of their kind and possibly not even of this earth (*Emaré*, 446–47).

Custance and Emaré are never *quite* assimilated. They remain a potential threat, *at the same time as* they are the lynchpin of dynastic – and, hence, national – security when they give birth to sons. These births, plus the figure of the mother-in-law in these two stories, spotlight a host of fears about ethnic, national and religious difference to explore what comprises collective identity. Proper kinship bonds knit up time and tie it to a masculine world order. The present exists only through the careful plotting of ancestors and antecedents. Time here is conceived as linear; the 'past' is always a story of origins and 'now' looks to its children to impel us into the future and erase the threat of death. The Man of Law's contempt for the Sultaness of Syria and for Donegild turns on this to point up masculine 'laws' of annexation and the purity of blood-lines. His accusation that the Sultaness harbours a 'mannish' desire to usurp power and lead the country ahead of her son (*Man of Law's Tale*, 434) overwrites the colonization of her country effected as part of the marriage contract between Custance and the Sultan. Though Custance brings an excellent dowry and the dynastic advantage of uniting Rome and Syria, the marriage requires that Syria surrenders its 'past', its Islamic laws and beliefs. The end result is national disorder, an uprising in which the Sultan is killed – and lineage broken – and Custance exiled (330–43, 348–57). Donegild also tries to preserve the old order, by interrupting the line of inheritance and Northumberland's future when she forges letters to claim that Custance has given birth to a demon – and, so, tainted the purity of their royal line (750–53). Her actions – condemned as full of "tyranny" – result in her death when she is denounced as a traitor to the family (696, 779, 781, 895. See also *Emaré*, 446–47, 529–40).

REVIEW

This section explores ideas about

- a range of identities – chivalric and 'masculine'; feminine; queer; religious; ethnic and national;
- how we narrate the 'self' through oppositions – public or communal vs. private; by naming and labelling; by attempting to secure boundaries between self and other, nation or religious identity and other;
- origins and foundational myths – family, kinship, birthright and inheritance AND the past: narratives of history, 'golden age' of Arthur and what this might mean for the present;
- chivalry and its anxious relation to the present;
- speech, silence and secrets;
- the multiple meaning of romance symbols and motifs like monsters;
- the shifting nature of time and space;
- how the intertextual nature of romance and its swirl of stories contributes to meaning.

READING

- Read *King Horn, Guy of Warwick* and/or *Richard Coeur de Lion.* What might these stories tell us about constructions of nation or Englishness?
- What might a reading of *Sir Degrevant* tell us about notions of class and matters of birthright?
- Read *Sir Gawain and the Carl of Carlisle, The Wedding of Sir Gawain and Dame Ragnell,* or any other Gawain analogues. How might these stories illuminate (or not) *Sir Gawain and the Green Knight?* More generally, for a detailed and accessible introduction to this poem read the chapter on *Sir Gawain* in J.J. Anderson (2005), *Language and Imagination in the Gawain-Poet.* Manchester: Manchester University Press.
- Read about Breton lays in Anne Laskaya and Eve Salisbury (eds.) 1995, 'General Introduction' in Laskaya and Salisbury (eds.) (1995), *The Middle English Breton Lays,* 1–13. How far do you agree with their definition of this type of romance story? What kinds of lays might not fit their description?

RESEARCH

- Extended research on theoretical concepts: for more on some of the theoretical ideas used in this section see the following:
  - for 'perverse dynamics' see Gail Ashton (2005), 'The Perverse Dynamics of *Sir Gawain and the Green Knight'* in *Arthuriana,* Vol. 15, No. 3, 51–74 and Jonathan Dollimore (1991), *Sexual Dissidences: Augustine to Wilde, Freud to Foucault.* Oxford: Clarendon Press;
  - for speech acts and naming, see Judith Butler (1997), *Excitable Speech: A Politics of the Performative.* New York and London: Routledge, 1–5, 29–35.
  - For medieval conceptions of time, space and history, see Jacques le Goff (1988), *The Medieval Imagination,* trans. Arthur Goldhammer. Chicago, IL: University of Chicago Press, 13; for modern notions of the same, see Julia Kristeva (1980), 'From one identity to another' in Leon S. Roudiez (ed.), trans. by Thomas Gora et al, *Desire in language: A Semiotic Approach to Literature and Art.* New York: Columbia University Press, 133–36). See also her 'Women's Time' and 'About

Chinese Women' in Toril Moi (1986), *The Kristeva Reader*.
Oxford: Blackwell, 190–92 and 187–213, respectively;

o for more on the Orpheus myth and on gender, see Robert
  Sturges (2001), *Chaucer's Pardoner and Gender Theory: Bodies
  of Discourse*. Houndmills and New York: Macmillan.

- What are the strengths and weaknesses of the above ideas, in
  your view? To what extent do theories like this illuminate or, conversely, hinder your reading of medieval romance? How might
  you use some of these ideas in other romances of your choice?
- Louise M. Sylvester (2008), *Medieval Romance and the Construction Of Heterosexuality*. Houndmills and New York: Palgrave
  Macmillan. Sylvester's innovation is to deploy both psychoanalytical theory and close linguistic analysis in her reading of a
  range of romances. How useful do you find her ideas?

PART THREE

WIDER CONTEXTS

CHAPTER 5

CRITICAL CONTEXTS

STARTING POINTS

Early scholars – those like Derek Pearsall, A.C. Spearing, David C. Benson and others – were often concerned with making value judgements on the literary merit of romance, with investigating philological and other linguistic matters, and with the provenance and editing of manuscripts. These are, of course, crucial interventions when part of any critical apparatus surely has to be an awareness of the medieval contexts in which romance was composed and circulated, as well as the difficulties these might pose for modern audiences. Middle English is, for example, integral to any context for medieval romance but is also a charged issue. There remains an insistence in some academic circles upon reading romance in its original 'English' which both elevates its academic status (by providing a challenge to its 'best' students) and perpetuates the notion of a difficult, even irreconcilable, medieval alterity. The danger of such a stance is that the most serious, self-perpetuating – and diminishing – audience for romance is always scholarly.

So, too, the academy has the last – indeed, sometimes the only – word on what kinds of texts we read and what kind of 'medieval' we construct. Those all-important contexts of romance are, thus, scripted through the accomplished, yet ultimately partial and partisan, lens of those who perpetuate certain, sometimes contemptuous, readings of this popular fiction; hence the commonplace academic currency, only recently dislodged by critics like Cohen and Weisl (see Cohen, 1999: 96–118 and Weisl, 1995: 70–84), that Chaucer's *Sir Thopas* in *The Canterbury Tales* is so 'bad' that it can only be a literary in-joke. Donald Sands is another instance of this trend. Rightly regarded for his edition of *Middle English Verse Romances* (1986), he dismisses important romance motifs as "tedious catalogues of trees, foods, clothes, weapons" (Sands, 1986: 6) to misread the ways in which romance signs itself and makes meaning. He remarks of another text that it is written by "an indifferent artist" and shows "no esthetic complexities, nor is it moral" (324).

All editorial decisions are, of course, vested ones that produce only partial 'readings'. Similarly teaching and research emphases skew our vision of medieval romance. This book, too, forecloses discussion when, constrained by space, I omit some romances and foreground others to present medieval romance in largely English terms. The academy has commendably brought 'lost' romance manuscripts to wider attention even as it is perhaps guilty of narrowing a horizon of expectations already circumscribed by issues about Middle English, the accessibility and availability of editions and an often yawning mismatch between academic study of romance and its vigorous afterlife in contemporary popular culture. Fortunately, a recent resurgence of academic interest in medieval romance from a range of innovative scholars goes a long way towards redressing some of these iniquities, with some outstanding edited collections of essays by Nicola McDonald (2004) and Corinne Saunders (2004) for example (see Further Reading, Key Texts), as well as innovative work from highly regarded theorists; it is to this that I now wish to turn.

KEY THEORISTS: DINSHAW, COHEN, INGHAM, DELEUZE AND GUATTARI, LINDLEY

Though I consider only recent theorists in this section, no discussion of key contributions to medieval romance study would be complete without passing mention of D.S. Brewer's seminal *Symbolic Stories* (1980). His extensive analysis of archetypal motifs, symbols, emblematic characters and formulaic plot structures in folklore, fairytale and romance foregrounds the family-drama scripts that still influence our readings today, mine included. Brewer describes, too, the coming-of-age plot so central to romance: an active hero – either expelled from the family unit or in ignorance of his origins – embarks on a quest for identity which is achieved only when he kills his rival, often monstrous, doubled self and wins the girl. Without early work of this kind, later critical interventions would lack their own foundation myths or stories of origins, and it is with this in mind that I begin my discussion.

Carolyn Dinshaw's contribution to medieval studies is inestimable. Her groundbreaking *Chaucer's Sexual Poetics* (1989) focuses on two analogous activities: how medieval thinkers wrote and interpreted texts (hermeneutics) and the ways in which we construct gender in both medieval and modern times. A medieval hermeneutics conceived the written text as the body of a captive woman. Its clothes are the letters that initially attract attention and seek to seduce, for this is a carnal body. As such, it must be 'glozed' or interpreted by a reader, usually a man, who can strip it of its letters, unveil it to expose its inner, allegorical meaning and re-clothe it as a 'proper' body, one whose truth is made subject to patriarchal law. In this sense, then, medieval literary theory is similar to the operations of a patriarchal world in which women are appropriated, exchanged and controlled by men. Dinshaw pushes this notion further and genders a reading activity that, she claims, is always bodily. To read the surface, literal letters of the text is to read like a woman (like, not as, for this is a subject position available to anyone regardless of the sex of its reader). This reading may be superficial at times, but it is also, in Dinshaw's view, more open to ambiguity. She describes the unveiling of its allegorical meaning as reading like a man: that is to seek closure and unequivocal, singular meaning.

Dinshaw applies these innovative notions to Chaucer's *Man of Law's Tale* and to Chaucer's work more generally. She explores the role of the narrator in the tale-telling contest that frames the *Tales* to argue that the Man of Law participates in a patriarchal traffic in women and texts, as when the merchants pass on 'tidings' about Custance (Dinshaw, 1989: 95). The narrator refuses to relate Custance's story as one of incest – as in other analogues – and so attempts to subject it to patriarchal ideology and the masculine law that he represents as a family lawyer. He works hard to define her as a suitably passive victim, suppressing not only the 'unkind abominations' of Dinshaw's chapter title, but any hint of female agency – hence his vehement excitement and insistence on divine intervention at moments when Custance might seem to slip the constraints of his story (90). Equally, the tale stresses exogamy and the role of the family in reproducing dominant organizations of power with the Man of Law condemning the Sultaness and Donegild as unnatural mothers, for example (92).

Dinshaw's more recent and supple theorizing about medieval texts takes us into queer and gender theory, as well as rethinking notions of history. *Getting Medieval* (1999) brings together the categories of "queerness, community, and history" to re-position them via an analysis of sex (Dinshaw, 1999: 144). She is interested in how we constitute a range of identities on the basis of sex, itself a complex and shifting set of categories, and especially in that medieval unspeakable known as sodomy, which she interprets as a range of same-sex *and* heterosexual acts and desires. Dinshaw argues that a community constitutes itself by expelling and policing what it regards as disorderly and, so, shores up normative, usually heterosexual, behaviours. Her examination of sexuality is read via queer theory, which seeks to dismantle taken-for-granted binaries like masculine–feminine and hetero-homosexual and seemingly natural norms. She does this through the 'touch of the queer' (see Dinshaw, 1995). 'Queer' might be a noun, a verb or an adjective. Its touch is a literal or figurative *making contact with* texts, discourses and histories, however partially, in order to make us look again at the unthinkable. This is the enterprise of 'getting medieval' in which history is conceived as discontinuous, an intersection of past and present.

Such an approach offers an interesting take on a romance genre that, she claims, invariably promotes heterosexuality. Despite these heterosexual imperatives, the genre is so profoundly marked by same-sex bonds that the heterosexual norms it presents are forever "haunted" by what is invariably excluded when we allow a heterosexual matrix to naturalize sex-gender-desire (Dinshaw, 1999: 12). Thus *Sir Gawain and the Green Knight* is about masculine identity (and also nationalism or Englishness, hence the framing device of an interlinked Trojan and English history (Dinshaw, 1997: 127). Dinshaw's discussion of *Sir Gawain* extensively details the erotic same-sex desire that charges all Gawain's dealings with Bertilak and his double the Green Knight. For Dinshaw, the graphic details of dismemberment in the hunt scenes parallel Gawain's figurative unravelling and atomization of his masculinity in the bedroom with the Lady while the kisses he exchanges with Bertilak are, as I also suggested in Part Two, queer and unsettling. So, too, she considers the role of the girdle crucial in the poem's attempt to undermine culturally determined behaviours like gender. For Dinshaw, though, the girdle is not a sinful symbol but precisely the means of Gawain's salvation. She argues that the Gawain-poet also uses the same term 'drurye' for 'girdle' in *Cleanness* where it alludes specifically to heterosexual relations. Thus, in *Sir Gawain* too, she says, it redirects same-sex and other illicit desires back into a heterosexual frame to recuperate Gawain's masculinity at the end.

Jeffrey Jerome Cohen is another key theorist in medieval studies. In *Of Giants* (1999) he reads a range of medieval romance texts via psychoanalytical theory. He chooses psychoanalysis for its concern to highlight and free up the "productive, disharmonious power" of contradictions, subversions and *jouissance* (Cohen, 1999: 70). He focuses upon bodies, often monstrous, and presentations of masculinity to explore ideas about gendered and national identities. Like Dinshaw, Cohen also employs queer theory to seek out indeterminacies rather than resolutions. One of the ways in which we see these processes at work, he believes, is in romance's obsession with the transhistorical phenomenon of the monster. Accordingly, he tracks literary representations of the giant in both medieval and contemporary texts. For Cohen, the giant embodies paradox. At once masculine with its excessive form and strength, it is also feminine being material and bodily: appetitive, sexually aggressive, associated with orality and images of a body in pieces. So, too, it is an 'other', banished to wildernesses yet forever haunting and threatening civilization and its spaces. Cohen suggests that we both fear and desire a monster who is the chivalric hero's unacceptable double. Thus romance returns to it time and again with its *gigantomachia* (traditional battle between the hero and the monster), a rite of passage to full sexual and social maturity. Often the giant is decapitated; a moment that Cohen claims asserts 'proper' heterosexual masculinity by expelling feminine "fleshly excess" and unacceptable same-sex desires (see 66–69). As such, the figure is a troubling example of a "cultural body on which the codes that produce a safely gendered identity have failed to adhere" (102).

Like Dinshaw (and others), Cohen explores *Sir Gawain and the Green Knight* in the light of what he calls its complex, humorous *and* sad presentation of the instability of gender. For him, the poem reveals how identity is a "repeated process of mourning" in which Gawain is finally unable fully to convey what his encounter with the Green Knight might have meant (see 143–52 and also 159–66 for discussion of its analogues). The most striking feature of his reading is that, unlike most other (including queer) theorists, Cohen concludes that "*any* performance of sexuality" is rendered impossible. Homosexuality may be written out in the Green Chapel but the heterosexuality it subsequently produces comes via "incoherence and failure" (150), and, so, can never be the hetero-normative 'correction' that most believe the poem to be.

The second strand of Cohen's discussion in *Of Giants* prefigures his later, equally influential contribution to medieval postcolonial studies. The monster's paradoxical nature, whereby it is both outside human society yet familiar and foundational to it, is integral to stories of origins – for nations, as well as for self. In psychoanalytical terms, the giant offers both a point of origin and – thanks to a fragile embodiment that always harks back to an imaginary completeness with the maternal body – a sense of loss (25). Thus we see it stories about our past like *Sir Gawain* and its analogues or in historiography such as Monmouth's *History of the Kings of Britain*. There we read of mythical times peopled by monsters defeated by heroes like Arthur and Brutus to colonize a place and give us a foundational romance or point of identification for a nation like England (10–12, 131–37 and 143–52. See Chapters 1–3 more generally). Cohen suggests that *Sir Gawain* is a poem of origins, a "prequel to the matter of Britain" (144) with a young Camelot, devoid of its history-to-come, as I argued in Part Two. Here the Green Knight is an unusual monster, neither one thing nor the other, a man-giant which means that he can "interrogate exactly where the difference between these modes of being resides" (145). For Cohen, the poem mingles game and violence and deforms a conventional *gigantomachia* scene by deferring its beheading. When the same creature is also Gawain's chivalric host, the monster is seen to inhabit the "secret interior" of courtly society and, hence, problematizes both gender and foundation myth (147).

Postcolonial theory demands that we re-conceptualize history. Western culture is usually constructed via a binary in which Eurocentric time and space colonizes and modernizes other more archaic temporal and geographical entities. In such thinking, 'medieval' becomes a pre-modern, 'primitive' alterity (the Dark Ages). This perspective sediments modernity as historical 'fact', a periodization that suggests history is linear and progressive. Many now challenge this view. They refuse an idea of 'medieval' as an originary fantasy or 'lost' origin for western culture. Instead, history is re-read through both its continuities *and* its ruptures. Cohen goes further to propose 'medieval' as a mid-point or in-between of historical time. Here he accepts that to some extent medieval *is* different from modern and, so, might be a point of origin for the modern world. Yet it is also, he argues, "an always-already existed alongside" (Cohen, 2000: 3), something both in *and out* of modernity because it is a moving point of friction rather than a fixed border (6). Thinking like this allows us to acknowledge the violent and difficult trauma that produces 'medieval' and concepts of, for example, 'nation', as well as repositioning 'medieval' as a problematic temporality that blurs "origin" and "end" (6).

Patricia Clare Ingham's contribution to medieval postcolonial studies is equally key to these debates about time, space and what 'medieval' might mean. Ingham concurs with Cohen's belief that although medieval alterity is important, it is neither clear-cut nor the sum total of postcolonial or modernist thinking. She argues that we should attend far more to the trauma and difficulties produced by cultural crises and sites of conquest within the medieval world (Ingham, 2003: 49–53). In this way, dominant 'universals' about nation, gender, class and ethnicity can be interrogated – through their similarities as much as their differences – as sites of conflict and ambiguity. Everything previously thought of as marginal – Saracens, Muslims, pagans, Jews, Wales, Ireland and so on – then becomes central in its own right, in a manoeuvre similar to the proximate dynamics I described in Part Two. So, too, identities and terms we take as given demand reconsideration; Cohen, for instance, extends the list of medieval postcolonial imperatives to include 'race', 'Christian', 'sexuality' and 'colonial' (Cohen, 2000: 6).

Both Cohen and Ingham are concerned with how we narrate the past. Ingham insists on the dismantling of convenient polarities in order to critique what appear to be homogeneous groups. Her methodology for this is organized around her groundbreaking idea of 'contrapuntal histories.' In musical notation, contrapuntal is a series of points running counter to the melody. In her postcolonial thinking, this contra or counter point becomes an additional set of histories inscribed over or under accepted ones. Through this, we might distinguish the *differences* of 'medieval' and 'modern', as well as analyse the more specific territories, contexts and unstable histories of medieval colonial rule which, when they *overlap*, offer a more indeterminate 'here' and 'there', 'then' and 'now' (Ingham, 2003: 458).

One of the enterprises of postcolonial theory is to dislodge historical grand narratives – and, too, the so-called master-texts of canonical writers. With this in mind, Ingham approaches Chaucer's *Man of*

Law's Tale in which ancient Rome with its foundational Christianity becomes a central image of colonialism at the expense of a demonized Islam (47–70). Ingham acknowledges that many critics have engaged with the tale's 'Orientalism' to recognize its melding of similarity and difference. Yet, she says, all finally offer readings which privilege Syria's alterity to England (59). For Ingham, such interpretations ignore the fact that history is not linear; what happens to Custance in Syria is repeated in England. The failed conversion of Islamic Syria becomes "an insular *reconversion*" when Custance converts Northumberland pagans to Christianity and thus shows how conquest demands repetition (60). Yet just as the unreliable narrator of the tale tells us something of the difficulties of recounting stories and histories as part of a colonial endeavour, so, too, laws and cultural markers shift across time and space (64–66). There is no clear binary in Chaucer's story between east and west. Instead, events repeat to give us a set of contrapuntal relations in which resemblances are as crucial as any differences. Thus Chaucer puns on Syria and 'Surrye'/England's Surrey, on Alla/Ali/Allah, and gives us Syrian Muslims, Syrian Christians, Roman and English Christians, English pagans and two seemingly opposed nations – England and Syria – subject to colonial Roman rule (60–63). Ingham also explores the presentation of women in the tale to demonstrate how Chaucer points up correspondences *and* differences *within* the Middle Ages and, so, slips any notion of a totalizing historical entity (65).

It may seem somewhat strange to end this discussion of key theorists with a brief consideration of the unique, challenging and rather diffuse ideas of the philosopher **Gilles Deleuze**. Deleuze is not a literary theorist and so does not directly work with texts but his innovations, which increasingly receive attention in medieval studies, bring together many of the strands of this section: concepts of history, time and space and what might be termed a queer unsettling of conventional hierarchies. He identifies two simultaneous movements in history: tracing and mapping. Tracing is the means by which we narrow down the past by selecting and ordering items in terms of their perceived importance. It has the effect of making the narratives of history seem stable or natural and helps them to fall into line with an idea of an over-arching masterplan or grand design. This is the conventional history of my previous discussions, a linear, progressive 'colonizing' of past events and moments. The other movement is what Deleuze calls mapping. This is an attempt to describe moments of 'libidinal excitement' – dialogues, experiments or conflicts in culture, which might occur when ideologies or systems both clash *and/or* mesh. For Deleuze and Guattari, his co-writer and fellow thinker, these moments are also occasioned when we reach a 'plateau'. Here, what is already in place can no longer exert power over what has so far been unrepresented, or silence it. The narratives of history and its dynamics of power thus always have something *more* to say to us than might first appear.

Mapping allows us both to accept the difference of the past *and* to open it up, to search for the possibilities of its 'within' and 'between'. As such, it bears consideration alongside the 'middle ground' of Cohen and Ingham, and the queer 'touches' through time of Dinshaw's discontinuous histories. Indeed, Deleuze and Guattari place the notion of 'middle' at the heart of their theoretical enterprise. Middle is the place where past/present, marginal/dominant or normative/aberrant can inter *and* intra-connect. It is not arrived at via binaries or oppositions, nor through a simple start-to-end progression. Instead, the middle is both reached and shaped by a series of flows that cut across, between, up, down, sideways and within ideas and hierarchies. This is an imaginary place and concept known as 'de-territorialization', somewhere ideas and silences can 'pick up speed' and swirl around rather than falling either side of a binary (like same/other or masculine/feminine). These flows also take us to 'milieux' or locations comprised of happenings, qualities and displacements rather than apparent certainties. These are energized by what the pair call 'rhizomatic connections.' Rhizomes are seeds in time, tiny, figurative bombs exploding at random which, in turn, give rise to those mappings, associations, flows and jumping-off points mentioned earlier.

Here, then, identities and concepts are always in the process of 'becoming' rather than simply 'being'. They do not merely dismantle binaries or invite us to look again at moments of rebellion or discord. Rather, they focus on asymmetries and contingencies, and make queer – because de-familiarized – connections (what they term 'machinic assemblages') without ever re-securing foundational norms like heterosexuality and, hence, connect up with Cohen's re-definition of 'queer'. How though might these ideas illuminate the stories and enterprises of medieval romance?

One example might be to rethink the part played by merchants in a story like the 'Man of Law's Tale.' We already know that Chaucer's tale works via a series of framing devices or unfolding miniatures.

I have argued that one of these frames concerns travel or locomotion, and in this the merchants are key. Like Custance, they are constantly in motion, plying a prosperous, global trade in spices and textiles (*Man of Law's Tale*, 133–40). They are fully invested in patriarchal structures, knitting up family, nation, law and faith when they inflate Custance's worth with superlative praise and pass on the singular, authoritative truth of her virtue – the "commune voys" – to the Sultan (155–68). They are also implicated in masculine 'tale-telling' and the circulation of story, spreading word of Custance *at the same time* as they offer merely rumour and non-scriptible 'Tidings' (181). In this respect, then, they disturb and exceed 'natural' categories of gender and the public order upon which such structures rest. So, too, they occupy their own 'middle' ground. The merchants plot the same kind of map as Custance: the real-life co-ordinates of east–west and European trading routes, and also the same in-and-out slippage of time and space. They, too, criss-cross seas and lands to draw the boundaries of the known world through their trade and seemingly settle nowhere. In this way, the merchants' queer energy corresponds to Custance's odd displacement and, so, enhances the tale's problem-atizing of concepts such as 'family' and 'nation'.

Floris and Blauncheflour is also marked by merchant activity with its subsequent disordering effect upon constructions of gender and nationhood. *Floris and Blauncheflour* continually undoes reductive binaries. To begin with, the merchants seem entirely masculine. They traffic in women and, like those in the *Man of Law's Tale*, write the world by staking an active claim to it via the footmarks they leave on established trading routes. They also buy Blauncheflour, happily giv-ing Floris's parents money and an engraved cup in exchange when they calculate her actual worth as far higher (*Floris and Blauncheflour*, 163–85). Blauncheflour is then sold on to the Emir of Babylon for his harem and at an inflated price too: for seven times her body weight (191–200).

Yet the merchants also draw a more feminine and shifting map – and with it an uneasy heterosexual script – through their shady deal-ings and perpetual motion. Their implicit silences and deceptions feed into the queer way in which Floris becomes an unlikely romance hero. When the merchants hand over the engraved cup, it is not really a legitimate exchange. One of them has stolen it from Caesar but says nothing, just as they fail to declare Blauncheflour's true worth when they buy her. That same cup is then given to Floris when he sets out on his quest to reclaim Blauncheflour. He pretends that he, too, is a merchant; though he is not always convincing, the guise allows him to re-trace the route the merchants took when they went with Blauncheflour to Babylon. The same sense of locomotion that drives the merchants also impels Floris. Floris travels from home to the innkeeper's dwelling in the east, on to the bridge-keeper and into the Emir's harem and Blauncheflour's bedroom, smuggled up in a basket of flowers. Each time, he closes down spaces, slips into them through guile or dialogue, by bartering and wagering money, cups and the engraved cup itself. In this oddly non-violent manner - there is no coming-of-age *gigantomachia* in this romance – Floris colonizes each space until he gains access to Blauncheflour's body ahead of the Emir. Once there, there is no conventional return home. Without the expected trajectory of exile-reconciliation, there is no real end-point to the family drama or re-securing of the kingdom. Instead, the Emir knights Floris, marries him to the Christian girl Blauncheflour and makes him his heir to keep his new-found surrogate 'children' in Babylon, held in time and space seemingly forever.

TOWARDS AN ENDING

Romance's persistence in popular culture paradoxically both undermines its literary status *and* keeps it fresh and vigorous. This split is seemingly consolidated in a conspiracy between academia and elements of the British tabloid press over the value of certain kinds of texts. English literature courses on popular fiction or media of all kinds often receive a disproportionate student take-up in universities. I suggest that this is precisely because most of its population consume such works in their leisure time *and* because of the 'illicit' thrill of studying *apparently* non-serious texts. The gap between what many people read for pleasure and what they regard as valuable for study is then sometimes taken up by hysterical media who scorn anything other than canonical, classical works. The study of popular fiction even occupies a conflicted place amongst scholars to a certain extent, at least according to a recent edition of the academic journal *Arthuriana*, with some Arthurian specialists concerned about how to position themselves and their work (see *Arthuriana*, Vol. 17, No. 4, Winter 2007).

Equally academic discourse neglects to talk about *pleasures* of texts though it is exactly this that impels most of us to study English literature in the first instance. Thus enjoyment somehow separates from matters of form, technique, effects and theories about texts. At the same time, popular culture deals in consumerism. Its audiences actively circulate, even alter it. Its forms and media are multiple, even ephemeral: print-based, films, TV series, games, fan-fiction, fanzines, web-based activities, toys and action figures. In this sense, contemporary popular romance, especially fantasy and sci-fi, intersects oral and written text cultures, just as many medieval romances did (Weisl, 2003: 17). As a result, its texts are unstable, its literary publishing history is diffuse, its sources and influences multiple and ever-changing and its aesthetics still a work in progress. So, too, those who decry the prolix and predictable style and structures of much romance may well miss the point. An academic obsession with print culture means that such features lose the impact they possess in oral performance, visual and digital media, and in medieval reading practices (as well as modern) where romance's generic emblems are freighted with meanings and associations. Equally, the repeated circulation of such apparently formulaic texts renders those same devices *more*, not less, meaningful or connotative. These issues impact upon scholars, students and readers of romance alike, all of whom are caught in its debates and tensions. In particular, texts of all kinds achieve mass circulation and exposure in contemporary culture via the very technologies ignored by some elements of a more academic readership.

One important way in which cult or popular status is enhanced is via the Internet. It is almost impossible to reference the proliferation of websites on medieval literature generally and medieval and modern romance more specifically, plus an array of often complex, interactive and highly informative official and author sites for the numerous films and TV series mentioned in this section – let alone the fanzines, fanbases, blogs and Wikipedia entries. Some of these sites are high status: those of the BBC, for example, or the .edu, ac.uk or .org sites. The medieval TEAMS texts online (Kalamazoo, University of Western Michigan) ensures that many medieval romances are readily available and complete with introductory and critical notes. Other websites are more populist or simply inaccurate. Most crucially of all, there are currently few reputable sites that deal exclusively with medieval romance. I note what I can in this constantly changing realm in the webography of the Further Reading section at the end of this book and take this opportunity to ask to what extent do we alter, even commodify texts when we sex them up for a digital, screen-obsessed twenty-first century? Is the enterprise in fact curiously medieval in spirit? Stories that began as oral renditions before moving to the mechanics of illustrated print manuscripts demanded new ways to recall, perform and interpret them – just as now we meld print and digital technologies to keep them shifting in an odd dynamics, at once competitive *and* synthesized. So, too, perhaps, both academic scholarship and a student readership must, then, accommodate its methodologies in order to confront texts that behave *differently* from those that it is used to, many of which will have 'cult' rather than literary status.

In this way, popular and academic responses might find a meeting point to ensure that romance is kept alive well beyond the lifetime of study guides like this one that capitalize upon a current resurgence of an interest I am loathe to see wane. So, too, a fresh approach might help to negotiate the dangers inherent in seeing the medieval past simply as a "palliative" to the here and now, both an historical reality *and* a constructed legacy (Weisl, 2003: 29). Of considerably less importance than how or what we study is, in my view, an examination of the capacious and slippery categories of romance to see "where we *live*" (Weisl, 2003: 31, emphasis mine). Perhaps then we might gain a fuller understanding of the ways in which we are still compelled by a genre that is at once coercive *and* transformative (Weisl, 2003: 153) and which still arouses such potent emotions and resonances.

CHAPTER 6

AFTERLIVES AND ADAPTATIONS

Northrop Frye's contention that medieval romance is the "structural core of all fiction" (Fry, 1976: 15) is now fairly commonplace academic currency. More recently, Nicola McDonald has described this medieval genre as the "ancestor" of many contemporary texts, both print and online (McDonald, 2004: 1). A cursory glance at contemporary, especially popular, culture certainly reveals a host of texts and associated cultural paraphernalia rooted in romance's structures and steeped in its motifs and emblems. There are modern love stories with their centrality of place, family connections and heterosexual marriage as social 'glue': Jane Austen, Eliot's *Middlemarch*, Joanna Trollope, Helen Fielding, Donna Tartt, Mills and Boon/Harlequin imprints, Gothic thrillers like Daphne du Maurier's *Rebecca*, historical romances like those of Philippa Gregory, through to Arthurian retellings and revisions, and on to UK BBC1 television series like *Doctor Who* plus films – *Lord of the Rings, Star Wars, Star Trek* – and their commercial spin-offs.

In short, medieval romance emerges in all genres of literature, in print, film and digital media, to lodge as some kind of collective memory or unconscious in popular culture, hundreds of years after its stories tracked their way in, out and across medieval contemporaneous texts. These medieval, so-called originals may yet be inaccessible, hidden within the academy, but somehow we still feel the pull of their strange worlds with their sense of loss and their simultaneously playful, distorted yet recognizable (un)realities. Romance's doubled strands – love and quest – both separate and intertwine to influence texts and media across temporal, geographical, linguistic and cultural spaces, producing a subtle and incomplete web of connections.

It can be no surprise that a genre steeped in oral traditions, performance or story telling and an early verse form finds its way into poetry, for instance. Medieval romance repeatedly questions and reconfigures ideas about love – both secular and spiritual – identities, histories and myth-making. Similar themes occupy poets from Spenser to Seamus Heaney. Spencer's *Fairie Queene* (1590, 1596, 1609) taps into romance's interest in the construction of nation and nationhood, drawing on medieval tales like *Sir Bevis of Hampton* to construct an allegorical, utopian other-world, an idyllic 'Gloriana' inspired by a perfection achieved through Elizabeth I. Similarly W.B. Yeats makes extensive use of Irish and Celtic romance tradition, in part to configure a nation state, 'Ireland'. Yeats borrows heavily from Middle Irish tales (1200 onwards) and Old-Irish Ulster sagas. Many of these recount the exploits of Cuchulain, whom Yeats deploys as the hero-spirit of all Ireland, and the story of Deirdre. Figures from Fenian cycles appear in his poems too (see Yeats: *The Wind among the Reeds,* 1899). Contemporary Irish poets like Seamus Heaney and Paul Muldoon also incorporate fantastic Irish stories and medieval legends in their work. Muldoon features tales of Deirdre, Cuchulain and Arthurian knights who all appear in the guise of figures from his own childhood while Heaney offers *Sweeney Astray* (1984), a translation of an Irish romance. Romance stories and motifs recur in Modernist poetry too, in Ezra Pound's use of classical tales, troubadour and minstrelsy and fertility myths, and T.S. Eliot's *The Wasteland* (1922). The latter recounts the story of an impotent fisher king ruling over a wasteland who can only be saved by the stranger-knight. Eliot's accompanying notes frequently refer to romance and myth as part of a wider redemptive tale of a twentieth century world devoid of spirituality.

CONTINUATIONS AND MEDIEVALISM

Certain romance texts or traditions have a particular and interesting longevity. *Guy of Warwick* is possibly a perfect example of romance's flourishing afterlife with the story seemingly adopted as a model of Englishness by a number of writers from William Copland (1569) onwards, and even taken up by a chapbook industry that printed small, cheap books and pamphlets for a mass audience during the eighteenth and nineteenth centuries. Chapbook accounts of *Guy* circulated alongside longer, more scholarly versions of the same tale. Many of these were taken to United States and North American colonies and the Continent by migrants who then produced their own accounts (Simons, 2004: 177–96). At the same time, during the first half of the nineteenth century, Sir Walter Scott was part of an active group of scholars, writers, editors and book collectors aiming to widen the readership of medieval romance. The collective believed that many medieval romance texts originated with and were circulated by Scottish minstrels. As such, their sponsorship sought to engage a national identity viewed as particularly pertinent during England's long war with Napoleon's France. George Ellis for instance published *Specimens of Early English Metrical Romances* (1805 onwards). Scott himself placed the visual and symbolic set-piece moments and quests for identity – all common romance features – at the heart of novels like *Rob Roy* (1817), *Ivanhoe* (1820) and the *Waverley* saga (1829–33).

Like many other stories of the Arthurian cycles, *Sir Gawain and the Green Knight* has fared particularly well in modern times. Translations include those by Brian Stone (Penguin, 1959), W.R.J. Barron (University of Manchester Press, 1974), Keith Harrison (Oxford, 1983), plus notable efforts by Marie Borroff (Norton, 1967) with its emphasis on rhyme, metre, and the alliterative patterning of the Middle English version, and the ornate language and diction of J.R.R. Tolkien's famous piece for Allen and Unwin (1975). Lately, both Simon Armitage and Bernard O'Donaghue have published contemporary versions of *Sir Gawain and the Green Knight* to testify to an invigorating and flourishing afterlife for romance even in the twenty-first century. O'Donaghue's is a scholarly yet accessible rendering (Penguin, 2006) but the best print translation in my view is Armitage's for Faber and Faber (2007/2008).

Armitage seems especially attracted by both the poem's heritage *and* its apparent neglect, a paradox that opens up a space for contemporary re-workings. Like many writers before him, he co-opts a text for an agenda that is at once transhistorical *and* firmly of a temporal reality, the *now*. He comments on the mythical qualities of *Sir Gawain and the Green Knight*, on its constantly evolving form that proves "eerily relevant" 600 years on, not least in its concern with our coexistence with the natural world. So, too, the poem belongs to a wider realm, to that esteemed category of 'English Literature' in whose crown it is "one of the jewels"; as such, the 'original' manuscript now resides in what Armitage believes to be its fitting home, the British

Library, London (Armitage, 2008: vii) where, he implies, it plays a crucial part in defining the qualities of a nation. The poem is, though, a relatively recent addition to an English Literature canon. Armitage notes its anonymous authorship and the way it languished for centuries, safe from the attentions of other 'greats' like Milton, Pope and Keats, and, thus, ripe for fresh approaches.

Armitage demonstrates a keen, somewhat nostalgic interest in *Sir Gawain and the Green Knight*'s particularities of place. The Gawain-poet was, like Armitage, a northerner. Armitage recognizes the geographical locations of *Sir Gawain and the Green Knight*, or, at least, the poem's strong sense of landscape. Accordingly, his translation seeks to "coax" the work over the Pennines and closer to his own particular home (vi). He recognizes, too, its Middle English dialect echoing in his own, present-day regional speech, the 'nobut' (nothing but) and 'barlay' (truce) of a declining generation (vii). Consequently, Armitage's supple and energetic translation focuses upon the language and sound of the poem to both invigorate and memorialize its vocabulary. In his Introduction, he states that his aim is for a "living" poem (viii). He rightly insists on retaining the alliterative pulse of what he calls its warp and weft, the way in which story and "sense" are directly located in its sound (viii). His refusal of a "crib" (ix) or a literal "tit-for-tat exchange of one language into another" (x) is fittingly medieval with its notion of translation as transformation (see Part One). It produces the "necessary flirtation" (ix) he hoped for, that careful balance of beauty, as in the description of Guinevere and "the quartz of the queen's eyes" (line 82) *and* contemporary colloquialisms: Arthur's knights are just "bum-fluffed bairns" (line 280) and the Green Knight holds the "mother of all axes" (line 208).

MEDIEVALISM AND VICTORIANISM

The afterlife of romance reaches a height during the Victorian age. Many texts of this time distinguish between romance and the novel. Their sub-titles – 'novel', 'history', 'romance' or 'tale' – point up issues of literary taste and aesthetic judgement. Any focus upon social reality, as in the nineteenth century classic novel, was perceived as a higher form. Such divisions are, however, less clear-cut than they seem. Rather, features of romance and its recurrent interests appear even in works claiming other allegiances and forms. From the 1880s, and on into the 1920s, many novels are what we now term 'imperial romances' – adventure or quest stories with a colonial setting. Most involve a journey, the testing of a central male protagonist, themes of exile and return, and exotic 'others' in the shape of peoples, nations, locations. They include books such as H. Rider Haggard's *King Solomon's Mines* (1885) and *She* (1905), H.G. Wells' *The Island of Dr Moreau* (1896), *The Time Machine* (1895), or *The War of the Worlds* (1898), and writers like Rudyard Kipling, Arthur Conan Doyle, and R.L. Stevenson. Such works emerge as part of a double impetus of overseas expansion and nostalgic colonialism and, once more, engage issues of national identities.

Perhaps the most crucial manoeuvre of the 1800s is Victorian England's general fascination with the Middle Ages, known as medievalism. The movement harks back to the interest of Romantic poets like Keats, Coleridge, Shelly and Byron in an idyllic, usually historically inaccurate past through which to accommodate the present. It turns to medieval romance, and, more specifically, to notions of chivalry and honour, hence the recurrence of an Arthurian tradition usually read through Malory's *Morte Darthur*. Helen Cooper cites Malory as the most continuously read author across the centuries, after Chaucer (though not as esteemed). She remarks the longevity and authority of a 1634 edition of the *Morte Darthur* which holds until two new versions in 1816. The story and its scenes were particular favourites for Victorian artists too (Cooper, 2004: 106).

Colonial incursions are, thus, set against an idealized 'medieval' past to flag a crisis of identity witnessed in Victorian texts and iconography. Some incorporate chivalric romance or fairy tales, either directly, as source material, and/or as a framing device – like an epilogue or a monologue – in a work identified as something else entirely. Victorian medievalism calls to mind the Pre-Raphaelites and Tennyson's poetry, *The Lady of Shalott* (1832), for example, or his rendering of the *Morte Darthur* at the end of his *Idylls* collection (1842). The Pre-Raphaelites brotherhood, founded in 1848, expanded in later years to give us notable participants such as William Morris, Algernon Swinburne, Edward Burne-Jones and Dante Gabriel Rossetti. Influenced by Scott and Keats, the group reproduced scenes from medieval texts as allegorical remedies against nineteenth century utilitarianism and commerce. At the same time, once again, their works mapped notions of nationhood and other identities by constructing a romantic, distant past (often Arthurian).

WOMEN AND ROMANCE

So far, my discussion has hinted at the split nature of romance's afterlife whose legacy is two strands of fiction: the fantasy-quest and the love story. Equally, our modern recycling of romance is sometimes an intellectual or artistic gesture that runs parallel to its denigration as a popular, less literary form. This paradox was at the heart of romance even in medieval times, as I suggested in Part One. It has continued down the centuries whereby romance is frequently disdained as a form for children and/or as suitable only for women. As well as those decrying lack of social realism in fiction, many writers and critics of the eighteenth and nineteenth centuries esteemed only irony, wit, parody, satire and an intellectual aesthetic as 'proper' literature. In contrast, romance was seen as low writing and the reading or writing of it as a debilitating, feminine pastime. Its female consumers were said to be especially susceptible to its inferior, if easy, charms on account of their hysterical, over-imaginative and uneducated sensibilities. Such antifeminist attitudes implicitly acknowledge romance's erotic or desiring undertones which render it at once dangerous (inciting illicit or irrational feelings) *and* highly seductive. Yet many influential authors adopted and adapted at least some aspects of the genre in works both popular and literary. Even those who are on record as condemning romance, like Samuel Richardson (*Pamela*, 1740 and *Clarissa*, 1747–48), take up some of its features for use in their work.

The mid-eighteenth century saw the emergence of Gothic romance, a hybrid strand melding medieval romance and French *roman* (long prose narrative). Possibly the first of these was Horace Walpole's *The Castle of Otrranto* (1764), which purports to translate a series of 1527 texts recounting an earlier medieval tale about the crusades. As ever, the development of Gothic romance seems embedded in social change and its attendant anxieties: a late 1700s self-emerging 'man' (mercantile, Protestant) set against an existing feudal-style system of property and inheritance rights. In literary terms, we recognize a long tradition of Gothic in dark tales of magic, demons, ghosts, secrets, terror and dislocation, and in writers as diverse as Ann Radcliffe (*The Mysteries of Udolpho*, 1794), Mary Shelley (*Frankenstein*, 1818 and 1831), Bram Stoker (*Dracula*, 1897), R.L. Stevenson (*Dr Jekyll and Mr Hyde*, 1886), Charlotte Bronte (*Jane Eyre*, 1847), Daphne du Maurier (*Rebecca*, 1938) and Anne Rice (the *Vampire Chronicles*, 1976 on).

There is no doubt, too, that Gothic romance seems especially attractive to women. Over 50 female authors wrote Gothic-style works between the 1790s and 1820s alone. This flourishing possibly allowed women access to a literary sphere formerly denied to them. Women's pleasure in romance – evidenced by modern sales figures – seemingly confirms it as a 'feminine' genre. Yet those same deep structures that appear so compelling for women equally attract male readers and writers. Rather, it may be that female authors and audiences negotiate the form differently. The competitive and heterosexual love triangle so central to all medieval romance may have a different resonance for men and women. Similarly, romance's drive to a happy heterosexual resolution incurs a social or cultural cost to both sexes. As such, according to many feminist and gender theorists, the stereotypical love-romances so derided in the academy and some elements of the media may actually play out cultural anxieties and traumas by re-scripting and reordering potential rape or violent scenarios. More generally, love romances straddle the history of the genre, whether chick-lit, Mills and Boon imprints, Jane Austen, Jeanette Winterson's melding of same-sex love, myth, legend and Arthurian romances (*The PowerBook*, 2001, *The Passion*, 1987, *Sexing the Cherry*, 1989, *Written on the Body*, 1992) or film: *Love Actually* (Richard Curtis, 2003) or Baz Luhrmann's *Moulin Rouge* (2001) amongst many others (see Pearce, 2004 and Pearce and Wisker, 1998).

FANTASY AND QUEST

Romance enjoys a prolific afterlife in sci-fi, fantasy and quest-oriented adventures. Many are Arthurian in scope and form. Often they replicate romance's interlaced or episodic structures, its supernatural elements, nostalgic pasts and dreamscapes, its visual concrete detailing set against broad brush-strokes or formulaic characterization and, of course, its dislocated worlds, fantastic tales of desire and loss, good and evil: Philip Pullman's *His Dark Materials* trilogy (1995–2000) and J.K. Rowlings' *Harry Potter* book series (1997–2007), C.S. Lewis's *Chronicles of Narnia*, Tolkien's Middle Earth sagas like the *Lord of the Rings*, or Mervyn Peake's *Gormenghast* trilogy (1946–59). The Victorian resurgence of interest in 'old' texts often took the shape of fantasy. George McDonald's *Phantasies* (1858) described itself as an adult fairytale, while the Brothers Grimm published their fairy tale collection in 1812–13. The lengthy Welsh romance-epic, the

Mabinogion, was translated into English in the mid 1800s by Lady Charlotte Guest. Other landmark texts include Lewis Carroll's *Alice* stories (1865/1872) and Bram Stoker's *Dracula* (1897), both of which have a flourishing afterlife in other media. *Dracula* – like *Frankenstein* – was adapted for the screen in 1931, for example, the first of many such versions.

The pulp fictions of fantasy adapt with especial ease to contemporary film, video games, and digital and visual media like the graphic novel. Early graphic novels give us romance in the twisted shapes of super-human hero-monsters reminiscent of the Green Knight like *Marvel* (first seen in 1939 comics), *Conan the Barbarian, Batman*, and *Superman* who was 'created' via a print and visual collaboration in 1938 between writer Jerome Siegel and artist Joe Schuster. These are romances with an edge, mass-produced and intentionally written for popular appeal with an economy we now recognize as intrinsic to popular texts. New media, graphic and digital appropriation of romance can also push language to its limits and distort reality to leave us with that de-familiarization so common in medieval romances. Tolkien's *Rings* sequence invents languages for its characters, for instance, while the special effects and computer-generated graphics of many modern films enhance all of these elements in films like Peter Jackson's *Lord of the Rings* series (2001–03), the *Chronicles of Narnia: The Lion, the Witch and the Wardrobe* (Andrew Adamson, 2005) and *Prince Caspian* (2008), *The Golden Compass* (Chris Weitz, 2007) or the *Harry Potter* franchise (2001 onwards).

ARTHURIAN LEGENDS

Modern re-workings of the Arthurian legend are too numerous to enumerate. Some of the most notable include T.H. White, *Sword in the Stone* (1936) and *The Once and Future King* (1958), Rosemary Sutcliff, *Sword at Sunset* (1963), Susan Cooper's *The Dark is Rising* series (1965–77), Marion Zimmer Bradley, *The Mists of Avalon* (1982) and Simon Hawke, *Wizard of Camleot* (1993). Other print fantasies that more loosely incorporate Arthurian figures or motifs, or else cross into historical fiction, comprise authors such as Lord Ernest Hamilton, *Launcelot* (1926), Edward Frankland, *Bear of Britain* (1944), Bernard Cornwell's *Warlord* chronicles (1995–97), Quinn Taylor Evans's *Merlin's Legacy* series (1996–99), Diana L. Paxson, *The Hallowed Isle, Book 2*: *The Book of the Spear* (1999), Gerald

Mann, *The Savage Damsel and the Dwarf* (2000), Jo Walton, *The King's Peace* (2000), Kevin Crossley-Holland, *Arthur: the Seeing Stone* (2000) and *Arthur at the Crossing Place* (2001).

Many offer fresh readings of this famous medieval story. Debra A. Kemp's *The House of Pendragon* series – *Book I: The Firebrand* (2003) and *Book II: The Recruit* (2007) – creates a lost daughter for Arthur and Guinevere called Lin. In these books, Lin recounts her autobiography to her son, Bear, and, in the second, her daughter. She tells of her life as a knight of the Round Table, her excellence at arms, how she is the victim of sexual abuse, violence, slavery and the contempt of familiar Arthurian figures like Mordred (son of Queen Morgause, Arthur's half-sister and his nemesis), Morgause and Guinevere. Teen and cross-over fiction also proves a popular home for Arthurian material, calling to mind works like Jan Fortune-Wood's *The Standing Ground* (2007), which reclaims the legend for Welsh historiography via a dystopian virtual world. Other young adult fictions include Karen Cushman's *Catherine, Called Birdy* (1994) and the award-winning *The Cross of Lead* by Avis Crispin (2002). Alternatively, US poet Margaret Lloyd's 2006 poetry collection, *A Moment in the Field: Voices from Arthurian Legend*, co-mingles Arthurian legend (largely sourced from Malory) and feminist perspective, while *Spamalot* (2005), a Broadway reworking of the comic 'Arthurian' film *Monty Python and the Holy Grail* (1975), continues to enjoy commercial success.

Perhaps not surprisingly given romance's strong visual detailing, film and TV also provide a seemingly natural home for Arthurian stories. In 2001, Kevin Harty counted approximately a hundred Arthurian-style films on general release (Harty, 2002). Recent additions to that list include Anthony Fuqua's *King Arthur* (2004) and *A Knight's Tale* (Brian Helgeland, 2001). The highly successful *Star Wars* franchise borrows heavily from Arthurian quest tradition, as do films such as Disney's *Shrek* (2001) or the cult TV series *Buffy the Vampire Slayer* and its spin-offs (1992 onwards); Buffy even pulls a sword from a stone in one early episode. *Star Wars* (the first trilogy 1977–1983, then returned in 1999 by a combination of popular appeal and clever marketing) includes six films plus prequels, a TV series plus its scripts, novels of screenplays, comics, Nintendo and role-playing *Star Wars* games, CD-ROMs, toys and action figures as part of a cult package that pervades popular culture and spotlights romance's contemporary relevance. Angela J. Weisl argues the *Star*

Wars story is firmly Arthurian. She rightly claims that it involves a quest, Jedi knights complete with their own code, reminiscent of Arthur's Round Table and mystical objects such as Luke Skywalker's light-sabre 'Excalibur'. Equally interesting is the fact that audiences of both traditions already know how their repetitive and episodic stories end (See Weisl, 2003: 183–207). More recently, the UK's BBC1 broadcast its thirteen part *Merlin* series (2008)) to acclaim, in spite of – or perhaps because of – its creaking, unrealistic sets and contemporary voices. Here a young Merlin and a boy-prince Arthur engage in a fresh and energetic coming-of-age story, negotiating all the usual plots and clandestine family connections with aplomb and verve.

SCI-FI AND CYBERSPACES

The commercial success of *Star Wars* points up a seemingly endless capacity for romance's regeneration, what Weisl accurately terms its 'persistence' in popular culture (Weisl, 2003: 19). In particular, science fiction and fantasy transform medieval romance for a contemporary world. Writers like Marge Piercy, Isaac Asimov, Russell Hoban, Ursula le Guin, Pat Robertson (*The End of the Age*, 1995) or Spider Robinson and Jeanne Robinson in *Star* trilogy (1991–95) all evidence anxiety about identities, border crossings and thresholds. The strange worlds of medieval popular fiction and its chivalric or faery-world objects recur in the liminal other-worlds of futuristic (yet pointing to the past) or imagined worldscapes complete with their own technologies and symbols, their colonizing impulses and permeable borders. The central figure of *Doctor Who* is a restless time traveller, forever on the move and without a home or resting place, for his own planet has been destroyed in the legendary Time War killing all his people. This cult BBC television series continually distorts time and space. In 'The Unquiet Dead' (Series 1, 2005) the Doctor tells his companion Rose Tyler that time is always in flux, never linear so that she can be born in the twentieth century yet still die in 1869. Episodes jump back and forth through time for, as Rose learns in the opening story of Series 1 ('Rose', 2005), the Doctor appears only at cultural or historical crisis points: Pompeii and the destruction of the Roman empire, the sinking of the 'Titanic', Kennedy's assassination, London 1941 at the height of the Blitz when family structures are destroyed and the mutated, lost children of a fictional Children's Plague demand of everyone they meet "Are you my mummy?" ('The Empty Child' and 'The Doctor Dances', Series 1, 2005). So, too, a growing, never directly acknowledged love story between the Doctor and Rose – whom he loses when he sends her into another time dimension in order to save her life at the end of Series 2 (2006) – crystallizes an undercurrent of loss that resonates in all his relationships with future companions.

Many of these sci-fi romances forge connections, not simply with their equally self-referential medieval counterparts (by reworking their stories and symbols) but within themselves. *Torchwood* spins off from *Doctor Who* with some of the leading protagonists switching between the two cult series; Captain Jack Harkness first appears in *Doctor Who's* previously mentioned 'The Empty Child' and tracks through several more episodes to be reanimated by Rose and gain immortal life when she inadvertently takes in the power of time from the Doctor's 'spaceship', the TARDIS. In later series of *Torchwood*, he is joined by Martha Jones, the Doctor's companion in Series 3 (2007). Equally, one of the Doctor's companions from previous series has her own children's TV series, the eponymous *The Adventures of Sarah-Jane Smith*. More generally, the Doctor is able to regenerate, thus giving us eleven different doctors so far from the series beginnings in 1963–1989 and its return to television in 2005 – with Christopher Ecclestone as the Doctor in Series 1, David Tennant in Series 2, 3 and 4 (2007–09) and Matt Smith in Series 5 (2010), plus a host of female companions. So, too, *Doctor Who's* use of arc stories compounds its deliberately wrought sense of intertextuality and aids its cult appeal. One of the best examples of this is the 'Bad Wolf' story which opens in Series 1 and continues through subsequent series. 'Bad Wolf' is a mystery bound up with the Doctor and manipulating his whole life, as well as his destiny with Rose. The phrase is seeded everywhere, in passing omens, graffiti, and the name of the TV game-show station (formerly 'Satellite 5', now 'Badwolf Corporation') that takes over the world in the final episodes of Series 1. Rose takes the words of this logo and spreads them across time and space when she accidentally incorporates the power of the time vortex in the TARDIS and learns how to see and read time. Thus, in 'The Parting of the Ways' (Series 1, 2005) she says "I am the Bad Wolf . . . I take the words. I scatter them . . . A message to lead myself here." The messages lead Rose and the Doctor to Norway and the fictional Bad Wolf Bay of a parallel 'Earth' where they finally part (Series 2, 'Doomsday', 2006).

Doctor Who is too typically a romance in its concern for origins. The Doctor's own identity, including his name and his regenerating, different faces, is complex and mysterious. At the heart of the character is a pervading sense of loss, both for his family and his people that draws others to him yet keeps him forever alone. Though he tries to deny the centrality of origins and all foundational myths – he claims not to 'do' family and tells Rose "This is who I am. Right here, now." (Series 1, 'The End of the World', 2005) – it remains integral to many of his stories. Episodes are intercut with the family scripts of his companions. Martha Jones, for example, leaves him in Series 3 to return to her own family after they have been endangered by events in another time and space, while Rose and her mother are finally reunited with her dead father in a parallel 'Earth' (Series 2 onwards).

The programme also writes a conflicted script for a sense of Englishness. It occupies a traditional, Saturday tea-time, family viewing slot that is nevertheless overlaid by an anti-establishment voice. The current series seemingly reclaims 'Arthurian' romance for the Welsh. Made by BBC Wales, some of its writers and actors are Welsh and the programmes are largely filmed in Cardiff (also the setting for *Torchwood* which is a secret, subversive institution sited on the time rift there). In an interview with Breakfast TV for the BBC, recorded in 2005 and part of the *Doctor Who Confidential* paraphernalia that accompanies the published DVD of Series 1, Christopher Ecclestone explains why he retained his own northern regional accent for the part of the Doctor. He comments on the Doctor's qualities of heroism and intelligence, something recognized from the series of his own childhood. These, he says, were for him and many others always associated with an alienating Received Pronunciation English. He wanted to reclaim the Doctor for a new generation by giving him a more vernacular voice of the people street-credibility – something that the subsequent Doctor, David Tennant, retains when he ditches his natural Scottish accent in favour of an indeterminate, semi-Estuary-speak. This impulse is augmented by pairing serious dramatic actors like Ecclestone and Tennant as the Doctor with unknown or celebrity companions: Billie Piper (Rose Tyler) is a former UK teen pop star while Catherine Tate (Donna Noble) is a popular cult comedienne.

The queer time–space contortions of sci-fi romances permeate these afterlives in a variety of ways. In 'The Temptation of Sarah-Jane

Smith' I and II (*The Sarah-Jane Smith Adventures*, transmitted 24 November and 1 December 2008 at 4.35 p.m. for BBC1, directed by Graeme Harper) Doctor's Who's former side-kick is enticed through a time fissure into a world from her past. The setting is a village fete in her birthplace, Foxgrove. The time is 1951, the very day that her parents were killed in an accident after the mechanical failure of their car, inexplicably leaving her three-month old self-abandoned in a pram at the side of the road. Sarah-Jane sees an opportunity to 'correct' time and so alter the course of the events that destroyed her family, even though she recognizes the trap the evil Trickster has sprung for her as part of his plans to annihilate Earth and build a world of his own.

Sarah-Jane's son, Luke, points out that if she alters time – something always contrary to the rules of this genre – then she affects the future which is in effect her past; she may not have him and will never meet the Doctor. In a parallel sequence, Luke's friend Rani has stumbled into the Trickster's future devastation of Earth. Her mother is one of the last surviving humans there but does not know Rani, for her 'past' has never taken place and she has never given birth to her. These space–time distortions allow characters to walk in and out of real and unreal worlds, to meet their past and future selves and to play with history and culture. In one incident, at the 1951 village fair, Sarah-Jane and Luke sign themselves as Victoria and David Beckham. Stories like these are attempts to grasp the ways in which past, future and present are contingent, constantly evolving narratives rather than realities, as well as explorations of love, loss and a search for completeness.

Finally, the Gothic-inspired fantasies of the *Batman* films offer their own unique takes on familiar romance scripts. The latest of these, Christopher Nolan's *The Dark Knight* (2007), sequel to *Batman Begins* (2005), offers an especially dark and compelling twist on traditional stories of origins. Here Gotham's commander of police, the Bruce Wayne/Batman figure, and Harvey Dent, Batman's 'White Knight', all join forces to rid the city of criminals and corruption. These three play by the rules to begin with, aware that even criminals have their own chivalric code of honour – at least until the Joker shows up. This is not the usual, half-in, half-out monster retaining some semblance of connection with humankind. Instead, the Joker is forever excluded because, as Batman realizes, human society has nothing he wants.

The value of kinship in securing order is clearly flagged in this film. The Joker circulates a family story that fails to secure identity. He initially claims that his father carved the smile into his face with a knife. He accuses his mother of the same deed on a subsequent occasion and then begins another version before abruptly declining to continue his tale. Later, he threatens the Commander's family, while the future – represented in the love triangle of Harvey Dent, Rachel and Bruce Wayne – is obliterated when Rachel dies. Her loss sends Batman deep into the shadows at the end as Gotham's 'Dark Knight', willing scapegoat for Dent's crimes as his monstrous alter-ego 'Two-Face'. Earlier, Batman's unethical attempts to save Rachel and Dent blow apart the remains of his own fractured family unit. He loses his childhood sweetheart Rachel and all hope of winning her back. His loyal manservant Alfred is left in limbo as Batman becomes the hunted, no longer the saviour of Gotham, while Lucius Fox, the mastermind and accomplice of Batman's real-life persona Bruce Wayne, resigns in despair to leave us with a chilling and bleak romance indeed.

Perhaps this, then, is the nature of post-modern romance: edgy, innovative, anxious and endlessly self-replicating, playful, obsessive, even a little camp, its theatricals and, above all, its search for utopias continuing to enthral us for years to come.

REVIEW

Chapter 5 explored

- a range of contemporary critical approaches: gender and queer, postcolonial, rhizomatic; and
- a range of key issues: notions of history, of time and space, bodies and gendered identities, religion, ethnicity, notions of nationhood.

Chapter 6 explored how medieval romance lived on

- in two strands: love dramas and fantasy/quest stories;
- in all genres and in a range of multi-media from print-based fiction, film, art, electronic games and CD-ROMs, in modernizations and translations, fanbases and fanzines, toys and other paraphernalia.

It examined, too, how adaptations and afterlives

- work out the same ideas as medieval romance: about identities, histories, space and time, stories of origins and colonizing impulses;
- use similar motifs and structures: exile and return, unknown strangers or lost birthright, symbols and technologies, concrete settings and other worlds, good and evil, focus on bodies.

READING

- Read Chaucer's 'Tale of Sir Thopas' in *The Canterbury Tales* and/or the 'Knight's Tale'. What kinds of romances are these? How might knowledge of Chaucer's place as a canonical English author affect our readings?
- Extend your knowledge of some of the issues raised in this section by reading at least two of the following: Helen Cooper (2004), 'Malory and the Early Prose Romances' in Saunders (ed.), *A Companion to Romance*, 104–20; Richard Cronin (2004) 'Victorian Romance: Medievalism' in Saunders (ed.), *A Companion to Romance*, 341–59; Kevin Harty (2001) 'Cinema Arthuriana: A Comprehensive Filmography and Bibliography', in Harty (ed.), *Cinema Arthuriana: 20 Essays*, Jefferson, NC: McFarland and Co., 252–302; Lynne Pearce and Gina Wisker (eds.) (1998), *Fatal Attractions: Re-scripting Romance in Contemporary Literature and Film*. London: Pluto; Lynne Pearce (2004), 'Popular Romance and its Readers' in Saunders (ed.), *A Companion to Romance*, 521–38; John Simons (2004), 'Chapbooks and Penny Histories' in Saunders (ed.), *A Companion to Romance*, 177–96; Angela Jane Weisl (2003), *The Persistence of Medievalism: Narrative Adventures in Contemporary Culture*. Basingstoke, UK: Palgrave Macmillan.
- Read Cohen's illuminating essay on *Sir Gowther* in Cohen (1999), 119–41 with its discussion of bodies, abjection and nationhood. How far do you agree with his comments? How might you use some of the ideas raised here in your reading of other medieval romances?
- Read Kathleen Davis (2000), 'Time Behind the Veil: The Media, the Middle Ages, and Orientalism Now' in Cohen (ed.),

The Postcolonial Middle Ages, 105–22. In what ways do her ideas bear reading with those of Ingham on the same tale?

- For more on the theories of Deleuze and Guattari read Glenn Burger (2003) *Chaucer's Queer Nation* (Minneapolis: University of Minnesota Press), i–xiii, 40–42. See also Deleuze and Guattari (1987), especially Chapter 1 and pp. 3–4, 12–13, 22–25.

RESEARCH

- What do you think McDonald means when she suggests that what makes romance popular is its "dangerous recreations" (McDonald, 2004: 16), and do you agree with her?
- What do you think might be at stake in some of the more abhorrent details of medieval romance stories with their seemingly anti- Semitic and xenophobic or racialized discourses?
- How do you account for the persistence of romance in popular contemporary culture?
- Choose ONE of the theoretical approaches discussed in this section and consider both its strengths and weaknesses. How might you use it in your own reading of medieval romance?
- Read Simon Armitage (2008) *Sir Gawain and the Green Knight*, London: Faber and Faber. Compare Armitage's engagement of ideas about language, a sense of Englishness, and monstrosity with those of the Gawain-poet.
- Read the collection of essays collated under 'The Round Table' in *Arthuriana* (2007), Vol. 17, No. 4, 93–116. How do you account for the tension between academic and popular 'versions' of romance? How might the two engage, in your opinion?
- Explore depictions of Jews and Jewishness in medieval romance. How do you account for their troubling persistence in texts long after they were expelled from England in the thirteenth century? What is at stake in their representation in romance? Starting point: read Sylvia Tomasch (2000), 'Postcolonial Chaucer and the Virtual Jew' in Cohen (ed.), *The Postcolonial Middle Ages*, 243–60.

FURTHER READING

Please see all Reading and Research at the end of each part of this book.

PRIMARY TEXTS

J.J. Anderson (ed.) (1996), *Sir Gawain and the Green Knight, Pearl, Cleanness, Patience*. London: J.M. Dent. All references to *SKKG* from this edition.

Geoffrey Chaucer, 'The Man of Law's Tale' in *The Canterbury Tales*. All references to this poem are from Larry D. Benson (1988), *The Riverside Chaucer*. Oxford: Oxford University Press and Houghton Mifflin Company.

Anne Laskaya and Eve Salisbury (eds) (1995), *The Middle English Breton Lays*. Kalamazoo: Medieval Institute Publications. All references to the following poems from this edition: *Sir Orfeo, Lay le Freine, Sir Degaré, Emaré, Sir Gowther*.

Maldwyn Mills (ed.) (1973), *Six Middle English Romances*. London: J.M. Dent.

Marijane Osborn (1998), *Romancing the Goddess: Three Middle English Romances About Women*. Urbana and Chicago, IL: University of Illinois Press.

Donald Sands (ed.) (1986 rep. 1997), *Middle English Verse Romances*. Exeter: Exeter University Press. All references to the following poems from this edition: *Sir Launfal, Floris and Blauncheflour. The Wedding of Sir Gawain and Dame Ragnell, Sir Gawain and the Carl of Carlysle*.

Eugène Vinaver (1990), *The Works of Sir Thomas Malory*, revised by P.J.C. Field. Oxford: Oxford University Press.

See also TEAMS medieval texts (print and online) sponsored by Medieval Institute, Kalamazoo: University of Western Michigan, www.wmich. edu/medieval/mip/mipubshome/html or Google TEAMS texts online.

KEY READING

Derek Brewer (1980), *Symbolic Stories: Traditional Narratives of the Family Drama in English Literature*. London: D.S. Brewer.

This is a foundational study of the motifs, archetypal figures, plots and structures of romance.

Jeffrey Jerome Cohen (1999), *Of Giants: Sex, Monsters, and the Middle Ages*. Minneapolis: University of Minnesota Press.

Cohen's groundbreaking work explores the many manifestations and significances of the monster in medieval romance texts of all kinds.

Jeffrey Jerome Cohen (ed.) (2000), *The Postcolonial Middle Ages*. Basingstoke: Palgrave Macmillan.

— (2000), 'Midcolonial' in Cohen (ed.), *The Postcolonial Middle Ages*, 1–18.

This excellent collection of essays confronts issues of time, space, and national identities in romance, as well as making major incursions into the emerging field of postcolonial studies.

Gilles Deleuze and Félix Guattari (1987), *A Thousand Plateaus: Capitalism and Schizophrenia* trans. Brian Massumi. Minneapolis: University of Minnesota Press.

This innovative and complex web of theoretical ideas about space, time, gender and history intersects the ideas of other key thinkers mentioned in this section.

Carolyn Dinshaw (1989), *Chaucer's Sexual Poetics*. Madison: University of Wisconsin Press.

— (1995), 'Chaucer's Queer Touches/A Queer Touches Chaucer' in *Exemplaria* 7.1: 75–92.

— (1997), 'Getting Medieval: Pulp Fiction, Gawain, and Foucault' in Dolores W. Frese and Katherine O'Brien O'Keefe (eds), *The Book and the Body*. Notre Dame and London: University of Notre Dame Press, 116–64. This is a fuller account of her take on *Sir Gawain* explored earlier.

— (1999), *Getting Medieval: Sexualities and Communities, Pre- and Postmodern*. Durham and London: Duke University Press.

— (2001), 'Pale Faces: Race, Religion, and Affect in Chaucer's Texts and Their Readers' in *Studies in the Age of Chaucer* 23, 19–41.

Dinshaw's outstanding contribution to medieval studies is witnessed in the range of critical innovations seen in these texts, as well as her detailed discussions of some key romance texts.

Rosalind Field (ed.) (1999), *Tradition and Transformation in Medieval Romance*. Woodbridge: Boydell and Brewer.

Field's scholarly yet accessible approach ensures that this collection of essays on medieval romance is both wide-ranging and innovative.

Patricia Clare Ingham and Michelle R. Warren (2003), *Postcolonial Moves: Medieval through Modern*. Basingstoke: Palgrave Macmillan.

Patricia Clare Ingham (2003), 'Contrapuntal Histories' in Ingham and Warren (eds), *Postcolonial Moves*, 47–70.

Ingham is another innovator in terms of critical approaches to medieval romance, something exemplified by both the chapter cited here and the collection of essays from a range of major theorists.

Roberta Krueger (ed.) (2000), *The Cambridge Companion to Medieval Romance*. Cambridge: Cambridge University Press.

— (2000) 'Introduction' in Krueger (ed.), *The Cambridge Companion to Medieval Romance*, 1–12.

Krueger's careful editing ensures that this is a major resource for medieval romance.

Nicola McDonald (ed.) (2004), *Pulp Fictions of Medieval England: Essays in Popular Romance*. Manchester: Manchester University Press.
This is an outstanding essay collection by virtue of both McDonald's provocative introduction and the lively collection of essays gathered here on a range of texts.
Ad Putter and Jane Gilbert (eds) (2000), *The Spirit of Medieval English Popular Romance*. Harlow: Pearson Education Ltd.
Ad Putter (2000), 'The Narrative Logic of *Emaré*' in Putter and Gilbert (eds), *The Spirit of Medieval Popular Romance*, 157–80.
Putter's accessible approach means that this collection – plus his round-up of romance's themes and motifs – is a valuable introduction to the field.
Raluca L. Radulesca and Cory James Rushton (eds) (2009), *A Companion to Popular Medieval Romance*. Cambridge: Boydell; D.S. Brewer.
This is another key collection that takes in a range of texts and critical approaches.
Corinne Saunders (ed.) (2004, rep. 2007), in Saunders (ed.), *A Companion to Romance From Classical to Contemporary*. Oxford: Blackwell.
Corinne Saunders (2004), 'Introduction' in Saunders (ed.), *A Companion to Romance*, 1–9.
— (2004), 'Epilogue: Into the Twenty-First Century' in Saunders (ed.), *A Companion to Romance*, 539–41.
Saunders offers some lively and interesting ideas in the introductory and concluding chapters of what is a fabulous resource for romance in all its many manifestations and afterlives.
The following academic journals also include many essays on romance in all its forms:
The Chaucer Review; Studies in the Age of Chaucer; Exemplaria; Arthuriana; PMLA; Journal of Early Modern and Medieval Studies.

OTHER READING

Elizabeth Archibald (2001), *Incest and the Medieval Imagination*. Oxford: Oxford University Press.
Susan Crane (1994), *Gender and Romance in Chaucer's Canterbury Tales*. Princeton, NJ: Princeton University Press.
Kathleen Davis (2000), 'Time behind the Veil: The Media, the Middle Ages and Orientalism Now' in Cohen (ed.), *The Postcolonial Middle Ages*, Basingstoke: Palgrave Macmillan, 105–22.
Sheila Fisher (1988), 'Leaving Morgan Aside: Women, History and Revisionism in "*Sir Gawain and the Green Knight*"' in Christopher Baswell and William Sharpe (eds), *The Passing of Arthur: New Essays in Arthurian Tradition*. NY and London: Garland, 129–51.
— (1989), 'Taken Men and Token Women in *Sir Gawain and the Green Knight*' in (eds) Sheila Fisher and Janet E. Halley, *Seeking the Woman in Late Medieval and Renaissance Writing: Essays in Feminist Contextual Criticism*. Knoxville: University of Tennessee Press, 71–108.

Northrop Frye (1957), *Anatomy of Criticism: Four Essays*. Princeton, NJ: Princeton University Press.

— (1976), *The Secular Scripture: A Study of the Structure of Romance*. Cambridge, MA: Harvard University Press.

John M. Ganim (2000), 'Native Studies: Orientalism and Medievalism' in Cohen (ed.), *The Postcolonial Middle Ages*, Basingstoke: Palgrave Macmillan, 123–34.

Thomas Hahn (1995), *Sir Gawain: Eleven Romances and Tales*

Phillipa Hardman (ed.) (2002), *The Matter of Identity in Medieval Romance*. Woodbridge: D.S. Brewer.

Geraldine Heng (1991), 'Feminine Knots and The Other in *Sir Gawain and the Green Knight*' in *PMLA* 106: 500–15.

— (2003), *Empire of Magic: Medieval Romance and the Politics of Cultural Fantasy*. New York: Columbia University Press.

Patricia Clare Ingham (2001), *Sovereign Fantasies: Arthurian Romance and the Making of Britain*. Philadelphia: University of Pennsylvania Press.

Timothy S. Jones and David A. Sprunger (eds) (2002), *Marvels, Monsters and Miracles: Studies in the Medieval and Early Modern Imaginations*. Kalamazoo: Medieval Institute Publications.

Arthur Lindley (1996), *Hyperion and the Hobbyhorse: Studies in Carnivalesque Subversion*. Newark, London: University of Delaware Press.

Barbara Tepu Lupack (ed.), *Essays on Arthurian Juvenilia*, New York: Palgrave Macmillan, 2004.

Richard Matthews (2004), 'Romance in Fantasy through the Twentieth Century' in Saunders (ed.), *A Companion to Romance*, 472–87.

Carol M. Meale (ed.) (1994), *Readings in Middle English Romance*. Cambridge: Cambridge University Press.

Corinne Saunders (1993), *The Forest of Medieval Romance: Avernus, Broceliande, Arden*. Cambridge: D.S. Brewer.

— (2001), *Rape and Ravishment in the Literature of Medieval England*. Cambridge: D.S. Brewer.

Angela Jane Weisl (1995), *Conquering the Reign of Femeny: Gender and Genre in Chaucer's Romances*. Cambridge: D.S. Brewer.

Judith Weiss, J. Fellows and M. Dickson (eds) (2000), *Medieval Insular Romance*. Cambridge: Cambridge University Press.

WEB RESOURCES

Textual resources

Electronic texts: Arthur

This offers a range of electronic texts on the Arthurian legend.

http://www.aloha.net/~mattman/electext.html

NLS Auchinleck MS

This site offers both facsimile and digital versions of the National Library of Scotland's Auchinleck manuscript. In addition to the full range of texts collated in this important medieval manuscript, it also has contextual and background information as well as bibliographical search facilities, accessed by both topic and text. It includes commentary on the physical state of the manuscript and its language, its significance, and editorial information – including a glossary of technical terms.

http://www.nls.uk/auchinleck

TEAMS Texts Online
This is a fantastic resource offering online access to a wide range of medieval texts, including romances, complete with a short introduction for each one. Its main site has some useful teaching and learning resources – reading lists, e-journals, news – available for students and teachers alike.

http://www.teamsmedieval.org/
http://www.teamsmedieval.org/texts/index.html

Vaughan's Auchinleck
Miceal Vaughan's introductory website about the Auchinleck manuscript offers illuminated manuscripts, some selective bibliographical and contextual material and related resources, including links to other useful manuscripts accessed via the 'Related Manuscripts' and 'Electronic Editions.' There is a good discussion of the Auchinleck manuscript and the 44 texts within it with comments on the form and state of each medieval manuscript and its modern editions.

http://faculty.washington.edu/miceal/auchinleck/

Medieval Images
Though this site is dedicated to English Mystery plays it is also an excellent, wide-ranging database of images from the medieval period which exemplifies its intertwined visual and literary culture and the material context of medieval textual production.

http://med-imag.english.cam.ac.uk

Introductory resources and searches

Andromeda
Jack Lynch's excellent index of literary resources has links to medieval documents of all kinds, illuminated manuscripts, the Voice of the Shuttle, and the Internet Medieval Sourcebook (Paul Halsall's primary resource for general medieval culture, currently being updated).

http://andromeda.rutgers.edu/~jlynch/Lit/medieval.html

Intute
This is a huge, free, searchable database for all kinds of subjects and topics aimed at both students and teachers. It has easy to use links to electronic journals, projects, timelines, manuscript studies and exhibitions, education and research.
    http://www.intute.ac.uk/artsandhumanities/browse

Labyrinth
This huge medieval resource contains a wealth of information from the general – armouring, chivalry, cosmology, medieval history, the Church – to more scholarly specifics such as manuscripts and Arthurian studies. It has clear and easy links to many other sites while its list of resources is outstanding.
    http://www.georgetown.edu/labyrinth/labyrinth-home.html

Luminarium
This outstanding resource offers a wealth of resources, which include essays and articles, timelines, biographies of many medieval writers, discussions, reading lists, images and links to some texts. It is especially useful for Malory and Chaucer.
    http://www.luminarium.org

NetSerf
This is an excellent introductory resource with dedicated sections for medieval culture, history, religion, women and one for Arthurian studies with contextual information on its literatures and stories.
    http://www.netserf.org

Voice of the Shuttle
Alan Liu's wide ranging resource is a powerful search engine with links to contextual information, numerous resources and critical material. Narrow the search by typing in 'medieval romance.'
    http://voc.ucsb.edu/browse

Other resources

Arthurnet
This offers numerous and easily accessible links to a range of sites including the Camelot Project, electronic romance texts, those concerned with the afterlives of the Arthurian legends, general medieval

context sites, reading lists, discussion groups and access to the scholarly journal *Arthuriana*. It also has some basic information on and background to Arthur's story.

http://www.clas.ufl.edu/users/jshoaf/Arthurnet.htm

The Camelot Project
This is a wide-ranging, multimedia introduction to Arthurian romance generally and, more specifically to *Le Chevalier de la Charrette* by Chrétien de Troyes. It has a full critical edition of the text plus links to others both medieval and modern and its afterlives, all with images, bibliographies and some contextual bites. It is particularly useful for information on symbols, motifs and the main characters of Arthurian legend, especially Gawain and Arthur. Its home page is easy to navigate with numerous links, plenty of basic information and helpful tips on how to use the search facilities to best advantage. The Project was devised by Alan Lupack and Barbara Tepa Lupack.

http://www.lib.rochester.edu/camelot/cphome.stm

Arthurian Resources
This has some useful bite-sized material on a range of topics including Arthurian afterlives in fantasy and sci-fi, plus links to the Camelot Project, for example, the scholarly journal *Arthuriana* and others.

http://www.jan.ucc.nau.edu/~jjd23/arthurian.htm

Arthurian Legend Home Page
Alan Baragona's reputable and highly useful site has many links to texts and information on the Arthurian legend and to scholarly projects in this field. It also has good bibliographies and a set of audio files.

http://academics.umi.edu/english/arthur.html

Siân Echard's Course Pages
This exceptionally valuable site is highly visual, packed with information and easy to navigate. It has many links to scholarly libraries and exhibitions and fabulous bite-sized information on King Arthur's legend: history, manuscript tradition, characters and major players, courtly love, afterlives. It also contains links to other manuscripts and writers: *Guy of Warwick,* The John Gower Page, Froissart, medieval Welsh poetry and prose, The Golden Cockerel edition of *Sir Gawain and the Green Knight*.

http://faculty.arts.ubc.ca/sechard/mypages.htm

Thomas Green's Arthuriana
This is a comprehensive survey of Arthurian history and its stories. It is especially good on Arthur's origins and the early tradition, especially in Wales, and also has some contextual information.
http://www.Arthuriana.co.uk

The Pendragon Society
This comprehensive and interesting site has a wealth of information – not all of it scholarly – in its own right, plus a host of links to other excellent, annotated resources accessed via its 'Quest'. It provides good bite-sized contexts for Arthur, Camleot, Merlin, some short articles and plenty for those new to the field.
http://www.pendragonsociety.org/webworld_quest_for_arthur. htm

David Wallace on Malory
This well-reputed resource based at the University of Pennsylvania contains several excellent readings of medieval works – including Chaucer's romances *Sir Thopas* and the *Knight's Tale* – plus a superb documentary on Malory's *Morte DArthur* by David Wallace for UK radio's BBC3 network (first broadcast 26 August 2007). Here Wallace explores the significance of the discovery of a manuscript of this text in 1934 in Winchester College. Not least, he urges us to rethink the context and implications of Caxton's 1485 edition which, until relatively recently, was the one used for all scholarly discussions and judgements.
http://writing.upenn.edu/pennsound/x/Wallace.html

Doctor Who
There are a number of linked sites for this series, all packed with information about characters, productions, the history of the series, images and video clips.
www.bbc.co.uk/doctorwho
www.bbc.co.uk/doctorwho/classic
www.bbc.co.uk/torchwood
www.thedoctorwhosite.co.uk/links.html

Arthuriana
This site is dedicated to the prestigious and wide-ranging scholarly journal *Arthuriana* edited by Bonnie Wheeler.
http://faculty.smu.edu/arthuriana/

Higher Education Academy
This outstanding resource offers material for teachers and students of literature of all kinds. It has a dedicated area for new projects, one of which is the creation of an online resource for medieval romance overseen by Raluca Radulescu at the University of Bangor and a team of medieval specialists. This will offer electronic versions of many texts complete with contextual 'bites' and supplementary information.

    http://www.english.heacademy.ac.uk

INDEX